TEACHER'S PET PUBLICATIONS

LITPLAN TEACHER PACK
for
Romeo and Juliet
based on the play by
William Shakespeare

Written by
Mary B. Collins

© 1997 Teacher's Pet Publications
All Rights Reserved

ISBN 978-1-60249-241-7

This **LitPlan** for William Shakespeare's
Romeo and Juliet
has been brought to you by Teacher's Pet Publications, Inc.

Copyright Teacher's Pet Publications 1997
11504 Hammock Point
Berlin MD 21811

Only the student materials in this unit plan
such as worksheets, study questions, assignment sheets, and tests
may be reproduced multiple times for use in the purchaser's classroom.

For any additional copyright questions,
contact Teacher's Pet Publications.

www.tpet.com

TABLE OF CONTENTS - *Romeo and Juliet*

Introduction	11
Unit Objectives	14
Reading Assignment Sheet	15
Unit Outline	16
Study Questions (Short Answer)	19
Quiz/Study Questions (Multiple Choice)	23
Pre-reading Vocabulary Worksheets	35
Lesson One (Introductory Lesson)	43
Nonfiction Assignment Sheet	46
Oral Reading Evaluation Form	50
Writing Assignment 1	53
Vocabulary Review Activities	56
Extra Writing Assignments/Discussion ?	58
Writing Assignment 2	64
Writing Assignment 3	67
Writing Evaluation Form	69
Unit Review Activities	70
Unit Tests	73
Unit Resource Materials	101
Vocabulary Resource Materials	115

ABOUT THE AUTHOR
WILLIAM SHAKESPEARE

SHAKESPEARE, William (1564-1616). For more than 350 years, William Shakespeare has been the world's most popular playwright. On the stage, in the movies, and on television his plays are watched by vast audiences. People read his plays again and again for pleasure. Students reading his plays for the first time are delighted by what they find.

Shakespeare's continued popularity is due to many things. His plays are filled with action, his characters are believable, and his language is thrilling to hear or read. Underlying all this is Shakespeare's deep humanity. He was a profound student of people and he understood them. He had a great tolerance, sympathy, and love for all people, good or evil.

While watching a Shakespearean tragedy, the audience is moved and shaken. After the show the spectators are calm, washed clean of pity and terror. They are saddened but at peace, repeating the old saying, "There, but for the grace of God, go I."

A Shakespearean comedy is full of fun. The characters are lively; the dialogue is witty. In the end young lovers are wed; old babblers are silenced; wise men are content. The comedies are joyous and romantic.

Boyhood in Stratford
William Shakespeare was born in Stratford-upon-Avon, England, in 1564. This was the sixth year of the reign of Queen Elizabeth I. He was christened on April 26 of that year. The day of his birth is unknown. It has long been celebrated on April 23, the feast of St. George.

He was the third child and oldest son of John and Mary Arden Shakespeare. Two sisters, Joan and Margaret, died before he was born. The other children were Gilbert, a second Joan, Anne, Richard, and Edmund. Only the second Joan outlived William.

Shakespeare's father was a tanner and glovemaker. He was an alderman of Stratford for years. He also served a term as high bailiff, or mayor. Toward the end of his life John Shakespeare lost most of his money. When he died in 1601, he left William only a little real estate. Not much is known about Mary Shakespeare, except that she came from a wealthier family than her husband.

Stratford-upon-Avon is in Warwickshire, called the heart of England. In Shakespeare's day it was well farmed and heavily wooded. The town itself was prosperous and progressive.

The town was proud of its grammar school. Young Shakespeare went to it, although when or for how long is not known. He may have been a pupil there between his 7th and 13th years. His studies must have been mainly in Latin. The schooling was good. All four schoolmasters at the school during Shakespeare's boyhood were graduates of Oxford University.

Nothing definite is known about his boyhood. From the content of his plays, he must have learned early about the woods and fields, about birds, insects, and small animals, about trades and outdoor sports, and about the country people he later portrayed with such good humor. Then and later he picked up an amazing stock of facts about hunting, hawking, fishing, dances, music, and other arts and sports. Among other subjects, he also learned about alchemy, astrology, folklore, medicine, and law. As good writers do, he collected information both from books and from daily observation of the world around him.

Marriage and Life in London
In 1582, when he was 18, he married Anne Hathaway. She was from Shottery, a village a mile from Stratford. Anne was seven or eight years older than Shakespeare. From this difference in their ages, a story arose that they were unhappy together. Their first daughter, Susanna, was born in 1583. In 1585 a twin boy and girl, Hamnet and Judith, were born.

What Shakespeare did between 1583 and 1592 is not known. Various stories are told. He may have taught school, worked in a lawyer's office, served on a rich man's estate, or traveled with a company of actors. One famous story says that about 1584 he and some friends were caught poaching on the estate of Sir Thomas Lucy of Carlecote, near Warwick, and were forced to leave town. A less likely story is that he was in London in 1588. There he was supposed to have held horses for theater patrons and later to have worked in the theaters as a callboy.

By 1592, however, Shakespeare was definitely in London and was already recognized as an actor and playwright. He was then 28 years old. In that year he was referred to in another man's book for the first time. Robert Greene, a playwright, accused him of borrowing from the plays of others.

Between 1592 and 1594, plague kept the London theaters closed most of the time. During these years Shakespeare wrote his earliest sonnets and two long narrative poems, 'Venus and Adonis' and 'The Rape of Lucrece'. Both were printed by Richard Field, a boyhood friend from Stratford. They were well received and helped establish him as a poet.

Shakespeare Prospers
Until 1598 Shakespeare's theater work was confined to a district northeast of London. This was outside the walls, in the parish of Shoreditch. Located there were two playhouses, the Theatre and the Curtain. Both were managed by James Burbage, whose son Richard Burbage was Shakespeare's friend and the greatest tragic actor of his day.

Up to 1596 Shakespeare lived near these theaters in Bishopsgate, where the North Road entered the city. Sometime between 1596 and 1599, he moved across the Thames River to a district called Bankside. There, two theaters, the Rose and the Swan, had been built by Philip Henslowe. He was James Burbage's chief competitor in London as a theater manager.

The Burbages also moved to this district in 1598 and built the famous Globe Theatre. Its sign showed Atlas supporting the world-hence the theater's name. Shakespeare was associated with the

Globe Theatre for the rest of his active life. He owned shares in it, which brought him much money.

Meanwhile, in 1597, Shakespeare had bought New Place, the largest house in Stratford. During the next three years he bought other property in Stratford and in London. The year before, his father, probably at Shakespeare's suggestion, applied for and was granted a coat of arms. It bore the motto Non sanz droict-Not without right. From this time on, Shakespeare could write "Gentleman" after his name. This meant much to him, for in his day actors were classed legally with criminals and vagrants.

Shakespeare's name first appeared on the title pages of his printed plays in 1598. In the same year Francis Meres, in 'Palladis Tamia: Wit's Treasury', praised him as a poet and dramatist. Meres's comments on 12 of Shakespeare's plays showed that Shakespeare's genius was recognized in his own time.

Honored As Actor and Playwright

Queen Elizabeth I died in 1603. King James I followed her to the throne. Shakespeare's theatrical company was taken under the king's patronage and called the King's Company. Shakespeare and the other actors were made officers of the royal household. The theatrical company was the most successful of its time. Before it was the King's Company, it had been known as the Earl of Derby's and the Lord Chamberlain's. In 1608 the company acquired the Blackfriars Theatre. This was a smaller and more aristocratic theater than the Globe. Thereafter the company alternated between the two playhouses.

Plays by Shakespeare were performed at both theaters, at the royal court, and in the castles of the nobles. After 1603 Shakespeare probably acted little, although he was still a good actor. His favorite roles seem to have been old Adam in 'As You Like It' and the Ghost in 'Hamlet'.

In 1607, when he was 43, he may have suffered a serious physical breakdown. In the same year his older daughter Susanna married John Hall, a doctor. The next year Shakespeare's first grandchild, Elizabeth, was born. Also in 1607 his brother Edmund, who had been an actor in London, died at the age of 27.

The Mermaid Tavern Group

About this time Shakespeare became one of the group of now-famous writers who gathered at the Mermaid Tavern in Cheapside. The club was formed by Sir Walter Raleigh. Ben Jonson was its leading spirit (see Jonson). Shakespeare was a popular member. He was admired for his talent and loved for his kindliness. Thomas Fuller, writing about 50 years later, gave an amusing account of the conversational duels between Shakespeare and Jonson:

"Many were the wit-combats betwixt him and Ben Jonson; which two I behold like a Spanish great galleon and an English man-of-war; Master Jonson (like the former) was built far higher in learning; solid, but slow, in his performances. Shakespeare, with the English man-of-war, lesser in bulk, but lighter in sailing, could turn with all tides, tack about, and take advantage of all winds, by the quickness of his wit and invention."

Jonson sometimes criticized Shakespeare harshly. Nevertheless he later wrote a eulogy of Shakespeare that is remarkable for its feeling and acuteness. In it he said:

> Leave thee alone, for the comparison
> Of all that insolent Greece or haughty Rome
> Sent forth, or since did from their ashes come.
> Triumph, my Britain, thou hast one to show
> To whom all scenes of Europe homage owe.
> He was not of an age, but for all time! . .
> . . . .
> Sweet Swan of Avon! what a sight it were
> To see thee in our waters yet appear,
> And make those flights upon the banks of Thames,
> That so did take Eliza, and our James!

Death and Burial at Stratford

Shakespeare retired from his theater work in 1610 and returned to Stratford. His friends from London visited him. In 1613 the Globe Theatre burned. He lost much money in it, but he was still wealthy. He shared in the building of the new Globe. A few months before the fire he bought as an investment a house in the fashionable Blackfriars district of London.

On April 23, 1616, Shakespeare died at the age of 52. This date is according to the Old Style, or Julian, calendar of his time. The New Style, or Gregorian, calendar date is May 3, 1616. He was buried in the chancel of the Church of the Holy Trinity in Stratford.

A stone slab-a reproduction of the original one, which it replaced in 1830-marks his grave. It bears an inscription, perhaps written by himself.

On the north wall of the chancel is his monument. It consists of a portrait bust enclosed in a stone frame. Below it is an inscription in Latin and English. This bust and the engraving by Martin Droeshout, prefixed to the First Folio edition of his plays (1623), are the only pictures of Shakespeare which can be accepted as showing his true likeness.

John Aubrey, an English antiquarian, wrote about Shakespeare 65 years after the poet's death. He evidently used information furnished by the son of one of Shakespeare's fellow actors. Aubrey described him as "a handsome, well-shaped man, very good company, and of a ready and pleasant smooth wit."

Shakespeare's will, still in existence, bequeathed most of his property to Susanna and her daughter. He left small mementoes to friends. He mentioned his wife only once, leaving her his "second best bed" with its furnishings.

Much has been written about this odd bequest. There is little reason to think it was a slight. Indeed, it may have been a special mark of affection. The "second best bed" was probably the one they used.

The best bed was reserved for guests. At any rate, his wife was entitled by law to one third of her husband's goods and real estate and to the use of their home for life. She died in 1623.

The will contains three signatures of Shakespeare. These, with three others, are the only known specimens of his handwriting in existence. Several experts also regard some lines in the manuscript of 'Sir Thomas More' as Shakespeare's own handwriting. He spelled his name in various ways. His father's papers show about 16 spellings. Shakspere, Shaxpere, and Shakespeare are the most common.

Did Shakespeare Really Write the Plays?
The outward events of Shakespeare's life are ordinary. He was hard-working, sober, and middle-class in his ways. He steadily gathered wealth and took good care of his family. Many people have found it impossible to believe that such a man could have written the plays. They feel that he could not have known such heights and depths of passion. They believe that the people around Shakespeare expressed little realization of his greatness. Some say that a man of his little schooling could not have learned about the professions, the aristocratic sports of hawking and hunting, the speech and manners of the upper classes.

Since the 1800's there has been a steady effort to prove that Shakespeare did not write the plays or that others did. For a long time the leading candidate was Sir Francis Bacon. Books on the Shakespeare-Bacon argument would fill a library (see Bacon, Francis). After Bacon became less popular, the Earl of Oxford and then other men were suggested as the authors. Nearly every famous Elizabethan was named. The most recent has been Christopher Marlowe. Some people even claim that "Shakespeare" is an assumed name for a whole group of poets and playwrights.

However, some men around Shakespeare-for example, Meres in 1598 and Jonson in 1623-did recognize his worth as a man and as a writer. To argue that an obscure Stratford boy could not have become the Shakespeare of literature is to ignore the mystery of genius. His knowledge is of the kind that could not be learned in school. It is the kind that only a genius could learn, by applying a keen intelligence to everyday life. Some great writers have had even less schooling than Shakespeare.

Few scholars take seriously these attempts to deprive Shakespeare of credit. Shakespeare's style is individual and cannot be imitated. Any good student recognizes it. It can be found nowhere else. Bacon is a poor candidate for the honor. Great as he was, he was certainly not a poet.

How the Plays Came Down to Us
Since the 1700's scholars have worked over the text of Shakespeare's plays. They have had to do so because the plays were badly printed, and no original manuscripts of them survive.

In Shakespeare's day plays were not usually printed under the author's supervision. When a playwright sold a play to his company, he lost all rights to it. He could not sell it again to a publisher without the company's consent. When the play was no longer in demand on the stage, the company itself might sell the manuscript. Plays were eagerly read by the Elizabethan public. This was even more true during the plague years, when the theaters were closed. It was also true during business depression. Sometimes plays were taken down in shorthand and sold. At other times, a dismissed actor would write down the play from memory and sell it.

About half of Shakespeare's plays were printed during his lifetime in small, cheap pamphlets called quartos. Most of these were made from fairly accurate manuscripts. A few were in garbled form.

In 1623, seven years after Shakespeare's death, his collected plays were published in a large, expensive volume called the First Folio. It contains all his plays except two of which he wrote only part-'Pericles' and 'Two Noble Kinsmen'. It also has the first engraved portrait of Shakespeare.

This edition was authorized by Shakespeare's acting group, the King's Company. Some of the plays in it were printed from the accurate quartos and some from manuscripts in the theater. It is certain that many of these manuscripts were in Shakespeare's own handwriting. Others were copies. Still others, like the 'Macbeth' manuscript, had been revised by another dramatist.

Shakespearean scholars have been determining what Shakespeare actually wrote. They have done so by studying the language, stagecraft, handwriting, and printing of the period and by carefully examining and comparing the different editions. They have modernized spelling and punctuation, supplied stage directions, explained difficult passages, and made the plays easier for the modern reader to understand.

Another hard task has been to find out when the plays were written. About half of them have no definite date of composition. The plays themselves have been searched for clues. Other books have been examined. Scholars have tried to match events in Shakespeare's life with the subject matter of his plays.

These scholars have used detective methods. They have worked with clues, deduction, shrewd reasoning, and external and internal evidence. External evidence consists of actual references in other books. Internal evidence is made up of verse tests and a study of the poet's imagery and figures of speech, which changed from year to year.

The verse tests follow the idea that a poet becomes more skillful with practice. Scholars long ago noticed that in his early plays Shakespeare used little prose, much rhyme, and certain types of rhythmical and metrical regularity. As he grew older he used more prose, less rhyme, and greater freedom and variety in rhythm and meter. From these facts, scholars have figured out the dates of those plays that had none.

Shakespeare As a Dramatist
The facts about Shakespeare are interesting in themselves, but they have little to do with his place in literature. Shakespeare wrote his plays to give pleasure. It is possible to spoil that pleasure by giving too much attention to his life, his times, and the problem of figuring out what he actually wrote. He can be enjoyed in book form, in the theater, or on television without our knowing any of these things.

Some difficulties stand in the way of this enjoyment. Shakespeare wrote more than 350 years ago. The language he used is naturally somewhat different from the language of today. Besides, he wrote in verse. Verse permits a free use of words that may not be understood by some readers. His plays are often fanciful. This may not appeal to matter-of-fact people who are used to modern realism. For all these reasons, readers may find him difficult. The worst handicap to enjoyment is the notion that Shakespeare is a "classic," a writer to be approached with awe.

The way to escape this last difficulty is to remember that Shakespeare wrote his plays for everyday people and that many in the audience were uneducated. They looked upon him as a funny, exciting, and lovable entertainer, not as a great poet. People today should read him as the people in his day listened to him. The excitement and enjoyment of the plays will banish most of the difficulties.

---- Courtesy of Compton's Learning Company

INTRODUCTION

This unit has been designed to develop students' reading, writing, thinking, and language skills through exercises and activities related to *Romeo and Juliet* by William Shakespeare. It includes twenty-one lessons, supported by extra resource materials.

The **introductory lesson** introduces students to Shakespeare and his times through a group research project. An additional introductory activity focuses on the theme of lost love, bringing the idea to date through "Dear Abby" letters. Following the introductory activity, students are given a transition to explain how the activity relates to the play they are about to read. Following the transition, students are given the materials they will be using during the unit. At the end of the lesson, students begin the pre-reading work for the first reading assignment.

The **reading assignments** are approximately thirty pages each; some are a little shorter while others are a little longer. Students have approximately 15 minutes of pre-reading work to do prior to each reading assignment. This pre-reading work involves reviewing the study questions for the assignment and doing some vocabulary work for some challenging vocabulary words they will encounter in their reading.

The **study guide questions** are fact-based questions; students can find the answers to these questions right in the text. These questions come in two formats: short answer or multiple choice. The best use of these materials is probably to use the short answer version of the questions as study guides for students (since answers will be more complete), and to use the multiple choice version for occasional quizzes. If your school has the appropriate equipment, it might be a good idea to make transparencies of your answer keys for the overhead projector.

The **vocabulary work** is intended to enrich students' vocabularies as well as to aid in the students' understanding of the play. Prior to each reading assignment, students will complete a two-part worksheet for approximately 10 vocabulary words in the upcoming reading assignment. Part I focuses on students' use of general knowledge and contextual clues by giving the sentence in which the word appears in the text. Students are then to write down what they think the words mean based on the words' usage. Part II nails down the definitions of the words by giving students dictionary definitions of the words and having students match the words to the correct definitions based on the words' contextual usage. Students should then have an understanding of the words when they meet them in the text.

After each reading assignment, students will go back and formulate answers for the study guide questions. Discussion of these questions serves as a **review** of the most important events and ideas presented in the reading assignments.

After students complete reading the work, there is a **vocabulary review** lesson which pulls together all of the fragmented vocabulary lists for the reading assignments and gives students a review of all of the words they have studied.

Following the vocabulary review, a lesson is devoted to the **extra discussion questions/writing assignments**. These questions focus on interpretation, critical analysis and personal response, employing a variety of thinking skills and adding to the students' understanding of the play.

The **group activity** which follows the discussion questions has students working in small groups to discuss the main themes of the play. Using the information they have acquired so far through individual work and class discussions, students get together to further examine the text and to brainstorm ideas relating to the themes of the play.

The group activity is followed by a **reports and discussion** session in which the groups share their ideas about the themes with the entire class; thus, the entire class is exposed to information about all of the themes and the entire class can discuss each theme based on the nucleus of information brought forth by each of the groups.

There are three **writing assignments** in this unit, each with the purpose of informing, persuading, or having students express personal opinions. The first assignment is to express personal opinions: students write a letter from Romeo or Juliet to Dear Abby and write Dear Abby's response. The second assignment is to inform: students take the information they have gathered through research, group work and class discussion and organize it into a composition. The third assignment is to persuade: considering guidelines suggested by an in-class speaker regarding dealing with emotional stress and death, and considering Juliet's personality and situation, students write a paper in which they detail how they would persuade Juliet not to commit suicide.

In addition, there is a **nonfiction reading assignment**. Students are required to read a piece of nonfiction related in some way to *Romeo and Juliet*. After reading their nonfiction pieces, students will fill out a worksheet on which they answer questions regarding facts, interpretation, criticism, and personal opinions. During one class period, students make **oral presentations** about the nonfiction pieces they have read. This not only exposes all students to a wealth of information, it also gives students the opportunity to practice **public speaking**. This nonfiction assignment is done in conjunction with the introductory research assignment.

The **review lesson** pulls together all of the aspects of the unit. The teacher is given four or five choices of activities or games to use which all serve the same basic function of reviewing all of the information presented in the unit.

The **unit test** comes in two formats: multiple choice or short answer, multiple choice, and composition. As a convenience, two different tests for each format have been included. There is also an advanced short answer version of the unit test.

There are additional **support materials** included with this unit. The **extra activities section** includes suggestions for an in-class library, crossword and word search puzzles related to the play, and extra vocabulary worksheets. There is a list of **bulletin board ideas** which gives the teacher suggestions for bulletin boards to go along with this unit. In addition, there is a list of **extra class activities** the teacher could choose from to enhance the unit or as a substitution for an exercise the teacher might feel is inappropriate for his/her class. **Answer keys** are located directly after the **reproducible student materials** throughout the unit. The student materials may be reproduced for use in the teacher's classroom without infringement of copyrights. No other portion of this unit may be reproduced without the written consent of Teacher's Pet Publications, Inc.

UNIT OBJECTIVES - *Romeo and Juliet*

1. Through reading William Shakespeare's *Romeo and Juliet*, students will explore the role of fate in life, the devastating effects of hate on both responsible and innocent parties, and the many facets of love.

2. Students will demonstrate their understanding of the text on four levels: factual, interpretive, critical and personal.

3. Students will analyze characters to better understand motivation for action.

4. Students will be exposed to background information about Shakespeare, Elizabethan drama, and *Romeo and Juliet*.

5. Students will examine Shakespeare's use of language.

6. Students will be given the opportunity to practice reading aloud and silently to improve their skills in each area.

7. Students will answer questions to demonstrate their knowledge and understanding of the main events and characters in *Romeo and Juliet* as they relate to the author's theme development.

8. Students will enrich their vocabularies and improve their understanding of the play through the vocabulary lessons prepared for use in conjunction with the play.

9. The writing assignments in this unit are geared to several purposes:
    a. To have students demonstrate their abilities to inform, to persuade, or
       to express their own personal ideas

Note: Students will demonstrate ability to write effectively to inform by developing and organizing facts to convey information. Students will demonstrate the ability to write effectively to persuade by selecting and organizing relevant information, establishing an argumentative purpose, and by designing an appropriate strategy for an identified audience. Students will demonstrate the ability to write effectively to express personal ideas by selecting a form and its appropriate elements.

    b. To check the students' reading comprehension
    c. To make students think about the ideas presented by the play
    d. To encourage logical thinking
    e. To provide an opportunity to practice good grammar and improve
       students' use of the English language.

10. Students will read aloud, report, and participate in large and small group discussions to improve their public speaking and personal interaction skills.

READING ASSIGNMENT SHEET - *Romeo and Juliet*

Date Assigned	Reading Assignment	Completion Date
	Act I	
	Act II	
	Act III	
	Act IV	
	Act V	

UNIT OUTLINE - *Romeo and Juliet*

1 Library	2 Nonfiction Reports	3 Dear Abby Materials Parts PV Act I	4 Film	5 Read Act I
6 Study ?s Act I Parts Act II PV Act II	7 Read Act II	8 Writing Assignment 1	9 Study ?s ?Act II Parts Act III PV Act III	10 Read Act III
11 Study ?s Act III Parts Acts IV & V PV Act IV & V	12 Read Acts IV & V	13 Study ?s Acts IV & V Vocabulary	14 Extra ?s Quotes	15 Writing Assignment 2
16 Group Activity	17 Reports & Discussion	18 Speaker	19 Writing Assignment 3	20 Review
21 Test				

Key: P = Preview Study Questions   V = Vocabulary Work   R = Read

STUDY GUIDE QUESTIONS

Thi page is left blank for two-sided printing.

SHORT ANSWER STUDY GUIDE QUESTIONS - *Romeo and Juliet*

Act I
1. Why do Sampson and Gregory fight with Montague's men?
2. Benvolio and Tybalt come upon the servants fighting. Contrast their reactions to the fight.
3. When Montague and Capulet enter and see the disturbance, they want to fight, too. What do their wives say?
4. What ended the opening skirmish?
5. Why is Romeo so sad?
6. In Act I Scene ii, Paris asks Capulet for Juliet's hand in marriage. What is Capulet's reply?
7. Why is Capulet giving a feast?
8. How does Romeo find out about the feast, and why does he decide to go even though (being a Montague) he is not invited?
9. Describe Juliet's relationship with her family in Act I.
10. At the end of Act I Scene iv, what does Romeo tell Benvolio, foreshadowing future action in the play?
11. What does Romeo mean when he says, "Oh, dear account! My life is my foe's debt"?

Act II
1. In Act II Scene ii, Romeo and Juliet profess their love for one another. Juliet is to contact Romeo (through a servant) the next day. Why?
2. Why does Friar Laurence agree to marry Romeo and Juliet?
3. What message does Nurse take to Juliet?
4. What warning does Friar Laurence give Romeo foreshadowing future events of the play?

Act III
1. In Act III, Mercutio and Benvolio get into a conflict with Tybalt. What does Romeo do when he comes upon them? Why? 2. How do Mercutio and Tybalt die?
3. What punishment did the Prince give Romeo for fighting?
4. Why did Romeo's killing Tybalt put Juliet in a bad position? What did she finally decide?
5. Lady Capulet goes to tell Juliet about the plans for the marriage between Juliet and Paris. What is Juliet's reaction?
6. What is Capulet's reaction when Juliet refuses to marry Paris?
7. What advice does Nurse give to Juliet?

Acts IV & V
1. Why does Juliet go to Friar Laurence's cell?
2. What plans do Friar Laurence and Juliet make?
3. What news does Balthasar bring Romeo? How does Romeo react?
4. What went wrong with the Friar's plan?
5. What are the circumstances of Paris' death?
6. After she wakes up from being drugged, why does Juliet kill herself with Romeo's dagger?

ANSWER KEY: SHORT ANSWER STUDY GUIDE QUESTIONS - *Romeo and Juliet*

Act I

1. Why do Sampson and Gregory fight with Montague's men?
    Sampson and Gregory are servants of the Capulet family, which has been feuding with the Montague family for quite some time. The feud has reached proportions involving all members and servants of both households.

2. Benvolio and Tybalt come upon the servants fighting. Contrast their reactions to the fight.
    Benvolio tries to break up the fight, but Tybalt wants to join in and kill all the Montagues.

3. When Montague and Capulet enter and see the disturbance, they want to fight, too. What do their wives say?
    Lady Capulet tells Capulet he'd better have a crutch instead of a sword, and Lady Montague tells her husband that he "shalt not stir one foot to seek a foe." The wives have had enough of the feud and wish their husbands, now old men, would stop fighting.

4. What ended the opening skirmish?
    The Prince threatened death to Capulet and Montague for disturbing the peace.

5. Why is Romeo so sad?
    He is love-sick, hopelessly in love with a girl who "hath sworn that she will still live chaste."

6. In Act I Scene ii, Paris asks Capulet for Juliet's hand in marriage. What is Capulet's reply?
    He says Juliet is too young (not yet fourteen), and Paris should wait two more years.

7. Why is Capulet giving a feast?
    He wants to bring out suitable bachelors for Juliet to meet so she may begin to choose a husband. Should Paris seem suitable to her after she has seen other men, Capulet would consent to the marriage.

8. How does Romeo find out about the feast, and why does he decide to go even though (being a Montague) he is not invited?
    Capulet's servant, unaware of Romeo's identity and unable to read, asks for help reading the invitation list Capulet has given him. Romeo wants to go because Rosaline will be there.

9. Describe Juliet's relationship with her family in Act I.
    She is a respectful young lady who obviously tries to please her parents if possible. They have a good family relationship.

10. At the end of Act I Scene iv, what does Romeo tell Benvolio, foreshadowing future action in the play?
"For my mind misgives/ Some consequence, yet hanging in the stars,/ Shall bitterly begin his fearful date/ With this night's revels, and expire the term/ Of a despised life closed in my breast/ By some vile forfeit of untimely death. . . ." (I.v,106-111)

11. What does Romeo mean when he says, "Oh, dear account! My life is my foe's debt"? He has learned that Juliet is a Capulet. His love for Juliet has brought him out of his depression, and for that he owes his enemy, a Capulet.

Act II

1. In Act II Scene ii, Romeo and Juliet profess their love for one another. Juliet is to contact Romeo (through a servant) the next day. Why?
She will get information about where and when they will be married.

2. Why does Friar Laurence agree to marry Romeo and Juliet? He hopes that it will help to end the feud between the families.

3. What message does Nurse take to Juliet?
She tells her to go to Friar Laurence's cell that afternoon to be married to Romeo.

4. What warning does Friar Laurence give Romeo, foreshadowing future events of the play?
"These violent delights have violent ends,/ And in their triumph die, like fire and powder/ Which as they kiss consume." He foreshadows the death of Romeo and Juliet.

Act III

1. In Act III, Mercutio and Benvolio get into a conflict with Tybalt. What does Romeo do when he comes upon them? Why?
He tries to defuse the situation and to get Tybalt to put his sword away. Tybalt is now his cousin by marriage, and Romeo does not wish to fight with him.

2. How do Mercutio and Tybalt die?
Mercutio is slain by Tybalt (under Romeo's arm), and Tybalt is slain by Romeo (avenging his friend's death).

3. What punishment did the Prince give Romeo for fighting?
The penalty was supposed to be death, but the Prince was lenient and exiled Romeo instead.

4. Why did Romeo's killing Tybalt put Juliet in a bad position? What did she finally decide?
She loved them both and is thrown into confusion as to whether to weep for Tybalt's death or Romeo's banishment. She decides to weep for Romeo.

5. Lady Capulet goes to tell Juliet about the plans for the marriage between Juliet and Paris. What is Juliet's reaction?
   She says she will not marry now but when she marries, Romeo will be her husband.

6. What is Capulet's reaction when Juliet refuses to marry Paris?
   He raves about her ungratefulness and tells her if she doesn't marry Paris, he will have nothing more to do with her.

7. What advice does Nurse give to Juliet?
   Nurse tells Juliet to marry Paris and try to forget Romeo, since he is probably permanently out of her life anyway.

Acts IV & V

1. Why does Juliet go to Friar Laurence's cell?
   She says she is going to make her confession, but actually she wants to get his advice.

2. What plans do Friar Laurence and Juliet make?
   They decide that Juliet should go home and agree to marry Paris, but that on the eve of her wedding she should drink a potion the Friar would make for her, a potion which will make her appear to be dead. After the potion wears off, she should go to Mantua to be with Romeo. The Friar will send word to Romeo of these plans.

3. What news does Balthasar bring Romeo? How does Romeo react?
   Balthasar tells Romeo of Juliet's death. Romeo rushes out to the apothecary to get poison. He goes to where Juliet has been placed so he can be with her when he drinks the poison.

4. What went wrong with the Friar's plan?
   His letters never got to Romeo; Romeo never found out that Juliet wasn't really dead.

5. What are the circumstances of Paris' death?
   Paris finds Romeo at the Capulet tomb and accuses him of killing Juliet with grief. Paris wants to fight; Romeo does not. Paris presses Romeo into fighting, and Romeo kills him.

6. After she wakes up from being drugged, why does Juliet kill herself with Romeo's dagger?
   She sees Romeo dead (from the poison) beside her, and decides to kill herself, too. Since there is no poison left, she uses his dagger.

MULTIPLE CHOICE STUDY GUIDE/QUIZ QUESTIONS - *Romeo and Juliet*

Act I

1. Why do Sampson and Gregory fight with Montague's men?
    a. Montague's men pushed Sampson against the wall.
    b. Gregory hurt one of the Montague women.
    c. They are fighting for their master, who is a Capulet.
    d. Montague's men wouldn't let them pass.

2. Benvolio and Tybalt come upon the servants fighting. How do they react to the fight?
    a. They both ignore it.
    b. Benvolio tries to break it up, but Tybalt wants to fight
    c. Benvolio wants to fight, but Tybalt runs away.
    d. They both encourage the servants to fight.

3. When Montague and Capulet enter and see the disturbance, they want to fight, too. What do their wives say?
    a. Let the servants do the fighting
    b. Join in the fight and help the men.
    c. The women want to fight too.
    d. The old men should stop fighting.

4. What ended the opening skirmish?
    a. The prince threatened them all with death if they fought.
    b. The Montagues wounded a Capulet servant.
    c. The Capulet servants got scared and ran away.
    d. Montague and Capulet told the servants to stop.

5. Why is Romeo so sad?
    a. He wanted to fight, but he missed it.
    b. The girl he loves does not want to get married.
    c. He had an argument with his cousin Benvolio.
    d. He just lost his best friend.

6. In Act I Scene ii, Paris asks Capulet for Juliet's hand in marriage. What is Capulet's reply?
    a. Paris needs more money to support her.
    b. Juliet does not want to marry anyone.
    c. Juliet's mother does not approve of Paris.
    d. Paris should wait two years until Juliet is older.

Study Guide/Quiz Questions - *Romeo and Juliet* - Page 2

7. Why is Capulet giving a feast?
    a. It is his wife's birthday
    b. He has just conquered the Montagues.
    c. He wants Juliet to meet suitable bachelors.
    d. He is celebrating the end of the fight with the Montagues.

8. Why does Romeo decide to go to the feast even though (being a Montague) he is not invited?
    a. Rosaline, the girl he loves, will be there.
    b. He wants to make peace with the Capulets.
    c. Benvolio offers to introduce him to Juliet.
    d. His favorite foods are going to be served.

9. Describe Juliet's relationship with her family in Act I.
    a. They have a good relationship. She tries to please her parents.
    b. She is very defiant. Her parents are angry with her.
    c. Her parents are too busy to pay attention to her.
    d. Juliet is afraid of them, because they are cruel to her.

10. At the end of Act I Scene iv, what does Romeo tell Benvolio, foreshadowing future action in the play?
    a. "If love be rough with you, be rough with love;
       Prick love for pricking, and you beat love down,
       Give me a case to put my visage in:
       A visor for a visor!..."
    b. "A torch for me: let wantons light of heart
       Tickle the senseless rushes with their heels,
       For I am proverbed with a grandsire phrase:
       I'll be a candleholder and look on.
       The game we ne'er so fair, and I am dun."
    c. "I mean, sir, in delay
       We waste our lights in vain, like lights by day.
       Take our good meaning, for our judgment sits
       Five times in that, ere once in our fine wits."
    d. "For my mind misgives
       Some consequence, yet hanging in the stars.
       Shall bitterly begin his fearful date
       With this night's revels, and expire the term
       Of a despised life closed in my breast.
       By some vile forfeit of untimely death."

11. What does Romeo mean when he says, "Oh, dear account! My life is my foe's debt"?
    a. Although the dinner was expensive, he didn't enjoy it.
    b. He is glad that Tybalt left the banquet without fighting.
    c. His love for Juliet has brought him out of his depression. Since she is a Capulet, he owes his enemy for his new happiness.
    d. He went to the party to get a glimpse of Rosaline. When he saw Rosaline dancing with another young man, he felt jealous and angry.

Study Guide/Quiz Questions - *Romeo and Juliet* - Page 4

Act II

12. In Act II Scene ii, Romeo and Juliet profess their love for one another. Juliet is to contact Romeo (through a servant) the next day. Why?
    a. He wants to send her some flowers. She will tell him where to send them.
    b. She will get information about where and when they will be married.
    c. She will tell him what time to come and meet her parents.
    d. He is inviting her to his house for dinner that night.

13. Why does Friar Laurence agree to marry Romeo and Juliet?
    a. Romeo offers him a lot of money.
    b. He doesn't like Paris, and doesn't think Juliet should marry him.
    c. He is obliged by the laws of the church to marry anyone who asks him.
    d. He hopes that it will help to end the feud between the families.

14. What message does Nurse take to Juliet?
    a. Romeo is ill and will not be able to meet her.
    b. They should wait a month and talk to their parents.
    c. She should go to Friar Lawrence's cell that afternoon to be married.
    d. Romeo will meet her in the garden again that night.

15. What warning does Friar Laurence give Romeo, foreshadowing future events of the play?
    a. "These violent delights have violent ends,
       And in their triumph die, like fire and powder
       Which as they kiss consume."
    b. "Young men's love then lies
       Not truly in their heart, but in their eyes."
    c. "Care keeps his watch in every old Man's eye,
       And where unbruised youth with unstuffed brain
       Doth couch his limbs, their golden sleep doth reign."
    d. "Come, come with me, and we will make short work:
       For, by your leaves, you shall not stay alone
       Till Holy Church incorporate two into one."

Study Guide/Quiz Questions - *Romeo and Juliet* - Page 5

Act III

16. In Act III, Mercutio and Benvolio get into a conflict with Tybalt. What does Romeo do when he comes upon them? Why?
    a. He remembers the Prince's warning about death to the fighters.
    b. Tybalt is now his cousin by marriage, and Romeo does not want to fight.
    c. Romeo knows Tybalt is too strong for them, and it would not be a fair fight.
    d. He has promised Friar Lawrence that he will never fight again.

17. How do Mercutio and Tybalt die?
    a. Romeo kills them both.
    b. Benvolio kills Mercutio, and Romeo kills Tybalt.
    c. Tybalt kills Mercutio, and Romeo kills Tybalt.
    d. Mercutio and Tybalt kill each other

18. What punishment did the Prince give Romeo for fighting?
    a. Death
    b. Exile
    c. Twenty years in jail
    d. A fine of 5,000 lira

19. For whom did Juliet decide to weep?
    a. Only Romeo
    b. Both Romeo and Tybalt
    c. Only Tybalt
    d. Neither of them

20. Lady Capulet goes to tell Juliet about the plans for the marriage between Juliet and Paris. What is Juliet's reaction?
    a. She says she will be glad to marry Paris if it pleases her parents.
    b. She says she has already married Romeo
    c. She says she will go to a convent and never marry.
    d. She says she will not marry now but when she does, she will marry Romeo.

21. What is Capulet's reaction when Juliet refuses to marry Paris?
    a. He raves about her ungratefulness and tells her if she doesn't marry Paris, he will have nothing more to do with her.
    b. He tells her he is glad to have a daughter who thinks for herself, and that she doesn't have to marry Paris.
    c. He banishes her to her room.
    d. He sends his guards to murder Romeo.

Study Guide/Quiz Questions - *Romeo and Juliet* - Page 6

22. What advice does Nurse give to Juliet?
    a. Ask her father to let her wait one year before she marries.
    b. Stand up for what she believes in.
    c. Forget Romeo since he is probably out of her life anyway, and marry Paris.
    d. Tell her father she has already married Romeo.

Study Guide/Quiz Questions - *Romeo and Juliet* - Page 7

<u>Acts IV & V</u>

23. Why does Juliet go to Friar Laurence's cell?
    a. She wants to have him annul her marriage to Romeo.
    b. She wants to go to confession.
    c. She has a letter for him to send to Romeo.
    d. She wants to get his advice.

24. What plans do Friar Laurence and Juliet make?
    a. They will tell Capulet the truth and ask him to beg the Prince to allow Romeo's return.
    b. Juliet should agree to marry Paris. On the eve of her wedding, she should drink a potion that will make her appear dead. After it wears off, she should go to Mantua to be with Romeo.
    c. She should threaten to kill herself if her father makes her marry Paris.
    d. The Nurse will help her disguise herself and run away that very night. They will go to another town. Friar Laurence will send Romeo there in a week.

25. What news does Balthasar bring Romeo? How does Romeo react?
    a. Balthasar tells Romeo where to meet Juliet and the Nurse. Romeo happily gets ready to leave.
    b. Balthasar tells Romeo that Juliet has married Paris. Romeo swears to return and kill Paris.
    c. Balthasar tells Romeo of Juliet's death. Romeo rushes out to the apothecary to get poison. He goes to Juliet's grave to drink the poison.
    d. Balthasar tells Romeo that Friar Lawrence has arranged for a pardon from the Prince. Romeo is free to return to be with Juliet.

26. What went wrong with the Friar's plan?
    a. The Prince changed his mind about the pardon.
    b. The potion was too strong and killed Juliet.
    c. The nurse would not cooperate.
    d. His letter never got to Romeo, so Romeo didn't know that Juliet was not really dead.

27. What are the circumstances of Paris's death?
    a. Capulet is angry that Juliet killed herself. He blames Paris, and kills him.
    b. Paris and Romeo meet at Juliet's tomb. Paris starts a fight, and Romeo kills him.
    c. Paris finds the remains of the potion that Juliet took. He swallows it and kills himself.
    d. Paris kills Romeo, and the Prince orders him to be killed.

Study Guide/Quiz Questions - *Romeo and Juliet* - Page 8

28. After she wakes up from being drugged, why does Juliet kill herself with Romeo's dagger?
    a. She sees Romeo dead from the poison. Since there is no poison left, she kills herself with his dagger.
    b. She realizes how foolish she had been, and she is afraid to be discovered by her father.
    c. She is still dazed by the potion. She picks up the knife and then trips, accidently killing herself.
    d. She is afraid the Prince will think she killed Romeo intentionally, and either banish her or put her to death.

ANSWER KEY - MULTIPLE CHOICE STUDY/QUIZ QUESTIONS
Romeo and Juliet

Act I	Act II	Act III	Act IV & V
1. C	12. B	16. B	23. D
2. B	13. D	17. C	24. B
3. D	14. C	18. B	25. C
4. A	15. A	19. A	26. D
5. B		20. D	27. B
6. D		21. A	28. A
7. C		22. C	
8. A			
9. A			
10. D			
11. C			

Thi page is left blank for two-sided printing.

PREREADING VOCABULARY WORKSHEETS

Thi page is left blank for two-sided printing.

VOCABULARY - *Romeo and Juliet*

Act I Part I: Using Prior Knowledge and Contextual Clues

Below are the sentences in which the vocabulary words appear in the text. Read the sentence. Use any clues you can find in the sentence combined with your prior knowledge, and write what you think the underlined words mean in the space provided.

1. Profaners of this neighbor-stained steel -/Will they not hear? What ho! You men, you beasts,

2. That quench the fire of your pernicious rage/With purple fountains issuing from your veins,

3. With tears augmenting the fresh morning's dew,/Adding to clouds more clouds with his deep sighs.

4. Black and portentous must this humor prove/Unless good counsel my the cause remove.

5. Why, such is love's transgression,/Griefs of mine own lie heavy in my breast,/which thou wilt prorogate, to have it pressed

6. Cuts beauty off from all posterity/She is too fair, too wise, wisely too fair

7. One desperate grief cures with another's languish.

8. Transparent heretics, be burned for liars!

9. Here in Verona, ladies of esteem/Are made already mother.

10. And what obscured in this fair volume lies/Find written in the margent of his eyes.

11. Too rude, too boisterous and it pricks like thorn.

12. On the forefinger of an alderman,/Drawn with a team of little atomies/Athwart men's noses as they lie asleep-

13. Then dreams he of another benefice/Sometime she driveth o'er a soldier's neck,

14. Thus from my lips by thine my sin is purged.

15. Too early seen unknown, and known too late!/That I must love a loathed enemy.

Romeo Vocabulary Act I Continued

Part II: Determining the Meaning

You have tried to figure out the meanings of the vocabulary words for Act I. Now match the vocabulary words to their dictionary definitions. If there are words for which you cannot figure out the definition by contextual clues and by process of elimination, look them up in a dictionary.

___ 1. profaners
___ 2. pernicious
___ 3. augmenting
___ 4. portentous
___ 5. transgression
___ 6. posterity
___ 7. languish
___ 8. heretics
___ 9. esteem
___ 10. obscured
___ 11. boisterous
___ 12. alderman
___ 13. benefice
___ 14. purged
___ 15. loathed

A. future generations
B. to dislike (someone or something) greatly
C. foreboding
D. to free from impurities
E. a member of the municipal legislative body
F. indistinctly heard; faint
G. evil; wicked
H. a church office endowed with fixed capital assets
I. to become weak or feeble
J. a violation of a law, command or duty
K. those who have irreverence for what is sacred
L. regard with respect
M. rough and stormy; violent
N. a person who holds controversial opinions
O. to make (something already developed) greater

Vocabulary - *Romeo and Juliet* Act II

Part I: Using Prior Knowledge and Contextual Clues

Below are the sentences in which the vocabulary words appear in the text. Read the sentence. Use any clues you can find in the sentence combined with your prior knowledge, and write what you think the underlined words mean in the space provided.

1. That were some spite. My <u>invocation</u>/Is fair and honest, and in his mistress' name

2. Arise, fair sun, and kill the <u>envious</u> moon,/Who is already sick and pale with grief

3. Her eye <u>discourses</u>, I will answer it.

4. Then twenty of their swords. Look thou but sweet,/And I am proof against their <u>enmity</u>,

5. Therefore pardon me,/And not <u>impute</u> this yielding to light love,/ Which the dark night hath so discovered.

6. And where the worser is <u>predominant</u>,/Full soon the canker death eats up that plant.

7. I pray thee, <u>chide</u> not. She whom I love now/Doth grace for grace and love for love allow.

8. To turn your households' <u>rancor</u> to pure love.

9. Why, is not this a <u>lamentable</u> thing

10. Is this the <u>poultice</u> for my aching bones?

11. I am the <u>drudge</u> and toil in your delight,/But you shall bear the burden soon at night.

Part II: Determining the Meaning - Match the vocabulary words to their dictionary definitions.

___ 1. invocation   A. most common or conspicuous
___ 2. envious   B. to express disapproval
___ 3. discourse   C. a person who does tedious, menial, or unpleasant work
___ 4. enmity   D. a soft, moist mass of bread, meal, clay or other substance
___ 5. impute   E. to attribute; credit
___ 6. predominant   F. an incantation used in conjuring
___ 7. chide   G. to narrate or discuss
___ 8. rancor   H. to express grief for or about
___ 9. lamentable   I. feeling, expressing or characterized by envy
___ 10. poultice   J. deep-seated, often mutual hatred
___ 11. drudge   K. bitter

Vocabulary - *Romeo and Juliet* - Act III

Part I: Using Prior Knowledge and Contextual Clues
   Below are the sentences in which the vocabulary words appear in the text. Read the sentence. Use any clues you can find in the sentence combined with your prior knowledge, and write what you think the underlined words mean in the space provided.

1. Doth much excuse the <u>appertaining</u> rage/To such a greeting.

2. Thou, wretched boy, that didst <u>consort</u> him here.

3. With thy black <u>mantle</u> till strange love grown bold/Think true love acted simple modesty.

4. So <u>tedious</u> is this day/As is the night before some festival/To an impatient child that hath new robes

5. Take up those cords. Poor ropes, you are <u>beguiled</u>,/Both you and I, for Romeo is exiled.

6. More <u>validity</u>,/More honorable state, more courtship, lives

7. Oh, how my heart <u>abhors</u>/To hear him named and cannot come to him,/
   To wreak the love I bore my cousin/Upon his body that hath slaughtered him!

8. Good Father, I <u>beseech</u> you on my knees,/Hear me with patience but to speak a word

Part II: Determining the Meaning
   You have tried to figure out the meanings of the vocabulary words for Act III. Now match the vocabulary words to their dictionary definitions. If there are words for which you cannot figure out the definition by contextual clues and by process of elimination, look them up in a dictionary.

___ 1. appertaining   A. to deceive by guile
___ 2. consort   B. well grounded
___ 3. mantle   C. to request earnestly
___ 4. tedious   D. a companion or partner
___ 5. beguiled   E. to belong as a proper function or part
___ 6. validity   F. moving or progressing very slowly
___ 7. abhors   G. to reject vehemently
___ 8. beseech   H. a cloak

Vocabulary - *Romeo and Juliet* - Acts IV & Act V

Part I: Using Prior Knowledge and Contextual Clues
   Below are the sentences in which the vocabulary words appear in the text. Read the sentence. Use any clues you can find in the sentence combined with your prior knowledge, and write what you think the underlined words mean in the space provided.

1. To stop the inundation of her tears,/Which, too much minded by herself alone,/ May be put from her by society.

2. I hear thou must, and nothing may prorogue it,/On Thursday next be married to this County.

3. Shall play the umpire arbitrating that/Which the commission of thy years and art Could to no issue of true honor bring.

4. For I have need of many orisons/To move the Heavens to smile upon my state,/ Which, well thou know'st, is cross and full of sin.

5. No, madam, we have culled such necessaries/As are behooveful for our state tomorrow.

6. But one thing to rejoice and solace in,/And cruel death hath catched it from my sight!

7. Our solemn hymns to sullen dirges change,/Our bridal flowers serve for a buried corpse,/ And all things change them to the contrary.

8. My dreams presage some joyful news at hand.

9. Noting this penury to myself I said,/"An if a man did need a poison now,

10. And here I stand, both to impeach and purge/Myself condemned and myself excused.

Part II: Determining the Meaning: Match the vocabulary words to their dictionary definitions.

____ 1. inundation   A. to gather; collect
____ 2. prorogue   B. destitution
____ 3. arbitrating   C. to challenge the validity of; try to discredit
____ 4. orisons   D. an omen
____ 5. culled   E. a prayer
____ 6. solace   F. to submit to settlement or judgment by arbitration
____ 7. dirges   G. to discontinue a session
____ 8. presage   H. to cover with water
____ 9. penury   I. a funeral hymn or lament
____10. impeach   J. comfort in sorrow

ANSWER KEY - VOCABULARY
Romeo and Juliet

Act I	Act II	Act III	Acts IV & V
1. K	1. F	1. E	1. H
2. G	2. I	2. D	2. G
3. O	3. G	3. H	3. F
4. C	4. J	4. F	4. E
5. J	5. E	5. A	5. A
6. A	6. A	6. B	6. J
7. I	7. B	7. G	7. I
8. N	8. K	8. C	8. D
9. L	9. H		9. B
10. F	10. D		10. C
11. M	11. C		
12. E			
13. H			
14. D			
15. B			

DAILY LESSONS

Thi page is left blank for two-sided printing.

LESSON ONE

Objectives
1. To gather background information
2. To give students the opportunity to fulfill their nonfiction reading assignment
3. To give students practice using the resources in the library
4. To distribute the materials which will be used in the unit

Activity #1
Distribute the materials which will be used in this unit. Explain in detail how students are to use these materials.

Study Guides Students should read the study guide questions for each reading assignment prior to beginning the reading assignment to get a feeling for what events and ideas are important in the section they are about to read. After reading the section, students will (as a class or individually) answer the questions to review the important events and ideas from that section of the play. Students should keep the study guides as study materials for the unit test.

Vocabulary Prior to reading a reading assignment, students will do vocabulary work related to the section of the play they are about to read. Following the completion of the reading of the play, there will be a vocabulary review of all the words used in the vocabulary assignments. Students should keep their vocabulary work as study materials for the unit test.

Reading Assignment Sheet You need to fill in the reading assignment sheet to let students know by when their reading has to be completed. You can either write the assignment sheet up on a side blackboard or bulletin board and leave it there for students to see each day, or you can "ditto" copies for each student to have. In either case, you should advise students to become very familiar with the reading assignments so they know what is expected of them.

Extra Activities Center The resource sections of this unit contain suggestions for an extra library of related books and articles in your classroom as well as crossword and word search puzzles. Make an extra activities center in your room where you will keep these materials for students to use. (Bring the books and articles in from the library and keep several copies of the puzzles on hand.) Explain to students that these materials are available for students to use when they finish reading assignments or other class work early.

Nonfiction Assignment Sheet Explain to students that they each are to read at least one non-fiction piece from the in-class library at some time during the unit. Students will fill out a nonfiction assignment sheet after completing the reading to help you evaluate their reading experiences and to help the students think about and evaluate their own reading experiences.

Books Each school has its own rules and regulations regarding student use of school books. Advise students of the procedures that are normal for your school.

<u>Activity #2</u>
Take students to your school library. Distribute the Research Assignment Sheet. Discuss the directions in detail, and give students ample time to complete the assignment. Depending on how quickly your students work, you may also need to spend part of the class period for Lesson Two in the library.

RESEARCH ASSIGNMENT - *Romeo and Juliet*

Purposes
1. To give you some background information about Shakespeare, *Romeo and Juliet* and the historical era in which the play was written and performed
2. To help you fulfill the nonfiction reading assignment which is a part of this unit

Assignment

Use the resources of your library and/or media center to find out as much as you can about the topic your group has been assigned. Take notes so you remember what you have read, seen or heard. After you have collected your information, get together with the other members of your group to compile a "Fact Sheet," an outline of the facts you have gathered. You will be asked to give an oral report to share your information with the rest of your classmates so that everyone in your class will have information about each of the topics assigned. The "Fact Sheet" you prepare will be the basis of your oral report and, if duplicated, will serve as a study guide for you and your classmates.

If you wish, you may use this assignment to fulfill your nonfiction reading assignment for this unit. If you choose to do so, be sure to fill out your Nonfiction Reading Assignment Sheet.

Group 1: Research Shakespeare. Pretend as if you had to write a book about Shakespeare (a biography). Include information about his personal life, professional life, important events and influences in his life, and any topics of controversy surrounding his life.

Group 2: Research British History 1550-1650. What was going on in Britain during the time just before, during and just after Shakespeare lived? Who were the rulers? What was the political atmosphere? What were the people concerned about? How did the people live? Answer these kinds of questions in your report.

Group 3: Research World History 1550-1650. What was going on in the rest of the world (besides Britain) during this period?

Group 4: Research *Romeo and Juliet*. What is the play about? Why is it famous? What do critics say about it? Has there been more than one version of the play? Which one(s) are most often performed? Why? Which is/was the best production of the play? What difficulties are there in performing the play (if any)?

Getting Started

There are many sources of information for your research. Books, periodicals (magazines & journals), films/filmstrips/videos, and encyclopedias are some of the most commonly used research materials. Each member of your group should use a different source of materials. For example, one member should look for books, another should look for articles in periodicals, etc.

NONFICTION ASSIGNMENT SHEET
(To be completed after reading the required nonfiction article)

Name _____ Date _____

Title of Nonfiction Read _____

Written By _____ Publication Date _____

I. Factual Summary: Write a short summary of the piece you read.

II. Vocabulary
    1. With which vocabulary words in the piece did you encounter some degree of difficulty?

    2. How did you resolve your lack of understanding with these words?

III. Interpretation: What was the main point the author wanted you to get from reading his work?

IV. Criticism
    1. With which points of the piece did you agree or find easy to accept? Why?

    2. With which points of the piece did you disagree or find difficult to believe? Why?

V. Personal Response: What do you think about this piece? OR How does this piece influence your ideas?

LESSON TWO

Objectives
1. To give students time to finish their research
2. To give students time to compile their fact sheets
3. To evaluate students' research
4. To have students share all the information they have found

Activity #1
Give students ample time to complete their research and compile their research fact sheets.

Activity #2
Have one student from each group give an oral report to the class summarizing the information all the group members found. If you choose, students could just listen instead of taking notes, and you could duplicate the fact sheets for distribution in the next class period. The other alternative is to have students take notes from the class reports so they have study materials.

Activity #3
Assignment: Have students cut out and bring "Dear Abby" letters from love-troubled readers from their newspapers for the next class period.

LESSON THREE

Objectives
1. To introduce the *Romeo and Juliet* unit in a more modern light
2. To assign reading parts for Act I
3. To do the prereading activities for Act I

Activity #1
Have students take turns reading their Dear Abby letters. (All letters should be related to troubled relationships.) NOTE: Bring several letters to class, too, especially if you can't count on your students to do this kind of assignment. Discuss the letters and Dear Abby's answers.

Activity #2
Transition: Tell students, in case they don't already know, that *Romeo and Juliet* is a story about two love-sick teenagers and their brief life together. Because it is a play, meant to be performed on stage and spoken orally, the reading will be done orally. Explain that each person in class will (eventually) have a speaking part to perform. The part does not have to be memorized, but the students' oral reading will be evaluated.

Make the reading part assignments for Act I, which will be read in Lesson Five. (Tell students the day and date that their reading will be done.)

Narrator (stage descriptions and directions; italicized)
Scene 1: Sampson, Gregory, Abraham, Benvolio, Tybalt, Capulet, Lady Capulet, Montague, Lady Montague, Prince, Romeo
Scene 2: Capulet, Paris, Servant, Benvolio, Romeo
Scene 3: Lady Capulet, Nurse, Juliet, Servant
Scene 4: Romeo, Benvolio, Mercutio
Scene 5: Servant 1, Servant 2, Servant 3, Capulet, Capulet 2, Romeo, Tybalt, Juliet, Nurse

Activity #3
Prior to reading Act I, students should preview the study questions and do the prereading vocabulary work for Act I. Give students the remainder of this class period to do the prereading work and, if they finish that, to begin practicing their oral reading parts.

LESSON FOUR

Objectives
1. To make it easier for students to understand the reading
2. To bring the text to life for students who may have difficulty understanding and visualizing the words

Activity
Show a film version of *Romeo and Juliet*.

LESSON FIVE

Objectives
1. To read Act I of *Romeo and Juliet*
2. To evaluate students' oral reading

Activity
Have students who were assigned to read parts for Act I do so during this class period. If you have not yet evaluated students' oral reading this marking period, this would be a good opportunity to do so. An Oral Reading Evaluation form is included in this unit for your convenience.

ORAL READING EVALUATION - *Romeo and Juliet*

Name _____ Class _____ Date _____

SKILL	EXCELLENT	GOOD	AVERAGE	FAIR	POOR
Fluency	5	4	3	2	1
Clarity	5	4	3	2	1
Audibility	5	4	3	2	1
Pronunciation	5	4	3	2	1
_____	5	4	3	2	1
_____	5	4	3	2	1

Total _____ Grade _____

Comments:

LESSON SIX

Objectives
1. To review the main events and ideas presented in Act I
2. To assign the speaking parts for Act II
3. To do the prereading work for Act II

Activity #1
Give students a few minutes to formulate answers for the study guide questions for Act I, and then discuss the answers to the questions in detail. Write the answers on the board or overhead transparency so students can have the correct answers for study purposes. Note: It is a good practice in public speaking and leadership skills for individual students to take charge of leading the discussions of the study questions. Perhaps a different student could go to the front of the class and lead the discussion each day that the study questions are discussed during this unit. Of course, the teacher should guide the discussion when appropriate and be sure to fill in any gaps the students leave.

Activity #2
Assign the following speaking parts for Act II. (Tell students that they will be reading Act II during the next class period.)

Narrator (stage descriptions and directions; italicized)
Scene 1: Romeo, Mercutio, Benvolio
Scene 2: Romeo, Juliet, Nurse
Scene 3: Friar Laurence, Romeo
Scene 4: Mercutio, Benvolio, Romeo, Nurse, Peter
Scene 5: Juliet, Nurse
Scene 6: Friar Laurence, Juliet, Romeo

Activity #3
Prior to reading Act II, students should preview the study questions and do the prereading vocabulary work for Act II. Give students the remainder of this class period to do the prereading work and, if they finish that, to begin practicing their oral reading parts.

LESSON SEVEN

Objectives
1. To read Act II of *Romeo and Juliet*
2. To evaluate students' oral reading

Activity
Have students who were assigned to read parts for Act II do so during this class period. If you have not yet evaluated students' oral reading this marking period, this would be a good opportunity to do so. An Oral Reading Evaluation form is included in this unit.

LESSON EIGHT

Objectives
1. To check students' understanding of the events of Act I and Act II
2. To tie-in the introductory activity
3. To give students a chance to practice writing in a letter format
4. To give students a chance to express their personal opinions
5. To give the teacher the opportunity to evaluate students' writing

Activity

Distribute Writing Assignment 1. Discuss the directions in detail and give students the remainder of this class period to complete this assignment.

LESSON NINE

Objectives
1. To review the main events and ideas presented in Act II
2. To assign the speaking parts for Act III
3. To do the prereading work for Act III

Activity #1

Give students a few minutes to formulate answers for the study guide questions for Act II, and then discuss the answers to the questions in detail. Write the answers on the board or overhead transparency so students can have the correct answers for study purposes. Note: It is a good practice in public speaking and leadership skills for individual students to take charge of leading the discussions of the study questions. Perhaps a different student could go to the front of the class and lead the discussion each day that the study questions are discussed during this unit. Of course, the teacher should guide the discussion when appropriate and be sure to fill in any gaps the students leave.

Activity #2

Assign the following speaking parts for Act III. (Tell students that they will be reading Act III during the next class period.)

Narrator
Scene 1: Benvolio, Mercutio, Tybalt, Romeo, Citizen 1, Prince, Lady Capulet, Montague
Scene 2: Juliet, Nurse
Scene 3: Friar Laurence, Romeo, Nurse
Scene 4: Capulet, Paris, Lady Capulet
Scene 5: Juliet, Romeo, Nurse, Lady Capulet, Capulet

Activity #3

Prior to reading Act III, students should preview the study questions and do the prereading vocabulary work for Act III. Give students the remainder of this class period to do the prereading work and, if they finish that, to begin practicing their oral reading parts.

WRITING ASSIGNMENT 1 - *Romeo and Juliet*

PROMPT

A few class periods ago you discussed some "Dear Abby" letters and you have read the first two acts of *Romeo and Juliet*. Now, your assignment is to write a "Dear Abby" letter from Romeo or Juliet (pick one) to Dear Abby (perhaps the current Dear Abby's ancestor!), and then write Dear Abby's response.

PREWRITING

Decide whether you want to write a letter from Romeo or from Juliet. Stop and think for a minute. Pretend you are Romeo (or Juliet). What is your problem? What does Abby need to know about your situation in order to give you advice? Jot down the things you need to include in your letter. Now, look at the things you have noted. Put them in a logical order that will make it easiest for Abby to understand your problem.

Now. Pretend you are Abby. You can clearly see the problem. What advice would you give? Jot down a few notes about things you would suggest. Go back and put them in a logical order so Romeo (or Juliet) will be able to understand your answer.

DRAFTING

Start with your letter from Romeo (or Juliet). Begin in a letter format using an appropriate date and with the traditional "Dear Abby" salutation. In a paragraph or two, give Abby a little background and explain your problem. Sign your letter with an appropriate pen name for Romeo (or Juliet).

For Abby's reply, again start with a letter format, an appropriate date, and the traditional "Dear [pen name]" salutation. In a paragraph or two, give your reply to Romeo (or Juliet). Close and sign your letter.

PROMPT

When you finish the rough draft of your letters, ask a student who sits near you to read it. After reading your rough draft, he/she should tell you what he/she liked best about your work, which parts were difficult to understand, and ways in which your work could be improved. Reread your paper considering your critic's comments, and make the corrections you think are necessary.

PROOFREADING

Do a final proofreading of your paper double-checking your grammar, spelling, organization, and the clarity of your ideas.

LESSON TEN

Objectives
1. To read Act III of *Romeo and Juliet*
2. To evaluate students' oral reading

Activity
Have students who were assigned to read parts for Act III do so during this class period.

LESSON ELEVEN

Objectives
1. To review the main events and ideas presented in Act III
2. To assign the speaking parts for Acts IV & V
3. To do the prereading work for Acts IV & V

Activity #1
Give students a few minutes to formulate answers for the study guide questions for Act III, and then discuss the answers to the questions in detail. Write the answers on the board or overhead transparency so students can have the correct answers for study purposes. Note: It is a good practice in public speaking and leadership skills for individual students to take charge of leading the discussions of the study questions. Perhaps a different student could go to the front of the class and lead the discussion each day that the study questions are discussed during this unit. Of course, the teacher should guide the discussion when appropriate and be sure to fill in any gaps the students leave.

Activity #2
Assign the following speaking parts for Acts IV & V. (Tell students that they will be reading Acts IV & V during the next class period.)

Act IV Narrator
  Scene 1: Friar Laurence, Paris, Juliet
  Scene 2: Capulet, Servant, Nurse, Juliet, Lady Capulet
  Scene 3: Juliet, Lady Capulet
  Scene 4: Lady Capulet, Nurse, Capulet, Servant 1, Servant 2
  Scene 5: Nurse, Lady Capulet, Capulet, Friar Laurence, Paris,
     Musician 1, Musician 2, Peter, Musician 3
Act V Narrator
  Scene 1: Romeo, Balthasar, Apothecary
  Scene 2: Friar Laurence, Friar John
  Scene 3: Paris, Page, Romeo, Balthasar, Friar Laurence, Juliet, Watchman 1,
     Watchman 2, Prince, Capulet, Lady Capulet, Montague

Activity #3
Prior to reading Acts IV & V, students should preview the study questions and do the prereading vocabulary work for Acts IV & V. Give students the remainder of this class period to do the prereading work and, if they finish that, to begin practicing their oral reading parts.

LESSON TWELVE

Objectives
1. To read Acts IV & V of *Romeo and Juliet*
2. To evaluate students' oral reading

Activity

Have students who were assigned to read parts for Acts IV & V do so during this class period.

LESSON THIRTEEN

Objectives
1. To review the main ideas and events from Acts IV & V
2. To review all of the vocabulary work done in this unit

Activity #1

Give students a few minutes to formulate answers for the study guide questions for Acts IV and V, and then discuss the answers to the questions in detail.

Activity #2

Choose one (or more) of the vocabulary review activities listed below and spend your class period as directed in the activity. Some of the materials for these review activities are located in the Vocabulary Resources section of this unit.

VOCABULARY REVIEW ACTIVITIES

1. Divide your class into two teams and have an old-fashioned spelling or definition bee.

2. Give each of your students (or students in groups of two, three or four) a *Romeo and Juliet* Vocabulary Word Search Puzzle. The person (group) to find all of the vocabulary words in the puzzle first wins.

3. Give students a *Romeo and Juliet* Vocabulary Word Search Puzzle without the word list. The person or group to find the most vocabulary words in the puzzle wins.

4. Use a *Romeo and Juliet* Vocabulary Crossword Puzzle. Put the puzzle onto a transparency on the overhead projector (or use your whiteboard), and do the puzzle together as a class.

5. Give students a *Romeo and Juliet* Vocabulary Matching Worksheet to do.

6. Divide your class into two teams. Use the *Romeo and Juliet* vocabulary words with their letters jumbled as a word list. Student 1 from Team A faces off against Student 1 from Team B. You write the first jumbled word on the board. The first student (1A or 1B) to unscramble the word wins the chance for his/her team to score points. If 1A wins the jumble, go to student 2A and give him/her a definition. He/she must give you the correct spelling of the vocabulary word which fits that definition. If he/she does, Team A scores a point, and you give student 3A a definition for which you expect a correctly spelled matching vocabulary word. Continue giving Team A definitions until some team member makes an incorrect response. An incorrect response sends the game back to the jumbled-word face off, this time with students 2A and 2B. Instead of repeating giving definitions to the first few students of each team, continue with the student after the one who gave the last incorrect response on the team. For example, if Team B wins the jumbled-word face-off, and student 5B gave the last incorrect answer for Team B, you would start this round of definition questions with student 6B, and so on. The team with the most points wins!

7. Have students write a story in which they correctly use as many vocabulary words as possible. Have students read their compositions orally! Post the most original compositions on your bulletin board!

LESSON FOURTEEN

<u>Objectives</u>
    1. To discuss *Romeo and Juliet* on interpretive and critical levels
    2. To discuss some significant quotations from the play

<u>Activity #1</u>

    Choose the questions from the Extra Discussion Questions/Writing Assignments which seem most appropriate for your students. A class discussion of these questions is most effective if students have been given the opportunity to formulate answers to the questions prior to the discussion. To this end, you may either have all the students formulate answers to all the questions, divide your class into groups and assign one or more questions to each group, or you could assign one question to each student in your class. The option you choose will make a difference in the amount of class time needed for this activity.

<u>Activity #2</u>

    After students have had ample time to formulate answers to the questions, begin your class discussion of the questions and the ideas presented by the questions. Be sure students take notes during the discussion so they have information to study for the unit test.

EXTRA WRITING ASSIGNMENTS/DISCUSSION QUESTIONS - *Romeo and Juliet*

<u>Interpretation</u>

1. What is the setting of *Romeo and Juliet*?

2. Where is the climax of the play? Explain your choice.

3. How much time passes during the play?

4. Think of a different title for the play. Explain your choice.

5. From what point of view is the play written? How does the point of view affect our perception of the story?

<u>Critical</u>

6. Define "tragedy" in the theatrical/literary sense of the word. Explain why *Romeo and Juliet* is a tragedy.

7. Are Romeo's actions believably motivated? Explain why or why not. Juliet's?

8. Was Juliet's disobedience to her father justified? Explain.

9. Evaluate William Shakespeare's style of writing. How does it contribute to the value of the play?

10. Describe Juliet's relationship with the nurse.

11. Describe Romeo's relationship with Mercutio.

12. Explain how William Shakespeare uses Friar Laurence in the play.

13. Explain the difference between being witty and being funny.

14. What things in *Romeo and Juliet* are due to fate, and what effect does that have on our perception of the play?

15. Are the characters in *Romeo and Juliet* stereotypes? If so, explain why William Shakespeare used stereotypes. If not, explain how the characters merit individuality.

Romeo Extra Questions Page 2

Critical/Personal Response

16. Could the same thing happen to two teenagers today? Explain why or why not.

17. Suppose Romeo and Juliet had not acted so hastily getting married. What effect, if any, would that have had on the play?

18. Had Juliet been older, do you think she would have done the same things she did in the play?

19. Suppose the Prince had made good on his first threat of death for breaking the peace and had not only banished Romeo. How would the story have changed?

20. Who is responsible for Romeo's death? Explain your answer.

22. Who is responsible for Juliet's death?

23. Discuss the importance and the role of these characters in *Romeo and Juliet*: nurse, Mercutio, Tybalt, and Paris.

Personal Response

24. Did you enjoy reading *Romeo and Juliet*? Why or why not?

25. Do you believe in "love at first sight"?

26. Do you believe dreams have meaning in our daily lives? Why or why not?

Quotations

1. What, drawn, and talk of peace! I hate the word   As I hate Hell, all Montagues, and thee. (I.i,77-78)

2. A crutch, a crutch! Why call you for a sword? (I.i,83)

3. If ever you disturb our streets again,
   Your lives shall pay the forfeit of peace. (I.i,103-104)

4. For my mind misgives
   Some consequence, yet hanging in the stars,
   Shall bitterly begin his fearful date
   With this night's revels, and expire the term
   Of a despised life closed in my breast
   By some vile forfeit of untimely death. (I.v,106-111)

Romeo Extra Questions Page 3

5. You will set a cock-a-hoop! You'll be the man! (I.v,84)

6. Oh, dear account! My life is my foe's debt. (I.v,120)

7. But soft! What light through yonder window breaks?
   It is the east, and Juliet is the sun! (II.ii,2-3)

8. O Romeo, Romeo, wherefore art thou Romeo? (II.ii,33)

9. That which we call a rose
   By any other name would smell as sweet. (II.ii,43-44)

10. Parting is such sweet sorrow (II.ii,184)

11. I have forgot that name and that name's woe. (II.iii,46)

12. In one respect I'll thy assistant be;
    For this alliance may so happy prove,
    To turn your households' rancor to pure love. (II.iii,90-93)

13. Alas, poor Romeo, he is already dead!
    Stabbed with a white wench's black eye, shot through the
    ear with a love song, the very pin of his heart cleft with
    the blind bowboy's butt shaft. (II.iv,12-16)

14. These violent delights have violent ends,
    And in their triumph die, like fire and powder
    Which as they kiss consume. (II.iv,9-11)

15. I do protest I never injured thee,
    But love thee better than thou canst devise
    Till thou shalt know the reason of my love. (III.i,71-72)

16. A plague o' both your houses! (III.i,111)

17. Oh, I am fortune's fool! (III.i,141)

Romeo Extra Questions Page 4

18. Ah, welladay! He's dead, he's dead, he's dead.
    We are undone, lady, we are undone.
    Alack the day! He's gone, he's killed, he's dead. (III.ii,36-38)

19. Wash they his wounds with tears. Mine shall be spent,
    When theirs are dry, for Romeo's banishment. (III.ii,130-131)

20. Affliction is enamored of thy parts,
    And thou art wedded to calamity. (III.iii,2-3)

21. ...thy wild acts denote
    The unreasonable fury of a beast.   . . .
    I thought thy disposition better tempered. (III.iii,110-115)

22. Romeo is coming. (III.iii,158)

23. Night's candles are burnt out, and jocund day
    Stands tiptoe on the misty mountaintops.
    I must be gone and live, or stay and die. (III.v,9-11)

24. Methinks I see thee, now thou art below,
    As one dead in the bottom of a tomb. (III.v,55-56)

25. Some grief shows much of love,
    But much of grief shows still some want of wit. (III.v,73-74)

26. Graze where you will, you shall not house with me. (III.v,190)

27. Delay this marriage for a month, a week;
    Or, if you do not, make the bridal bed
    In that dim monument where Tybalt lies. (III.v,201-203)

28. My dismal scene I needs must act alone.
    Come vial. (IV.iii,19-20)

29. Death is my son-in-law, Death is my heir (IV.v,38)

30. I dreamed my lady came and found me dead -- (V.i,6)

31. Well, Juliet, I will lie with thee tonight. (V.i,34)

Romeo Extra Questions Page 5

32. Good gentle youth, tempt not a desperate man.
    Fly hence and leave me. (V.iii,59-60)

33. How oft when men are at the point of death
    Have they been merry! Which their keepers call
    A lightning before death. (V.iii,88-90)

34. Capulet! Montague!
    See what a scourge is laid upon your hate
    That Heaven finds means to kill your joys with love!
    And I, for winking at your discords too,
    Have lost a brace of kinsmen. All are punished. (V.iii,291-295)

LESSON FIFTEEN

<u>Objectives</u>
    1. To give students practice writing to inform
    2. To review
    3. To give the teacher the opportunity to evaluate students' writing

<u>Activity</u>
    Distribute Writing Assignment 2. Discuss the directions in detail and give students this class period to do the assignment.

    <u>Follow - Up:</u> After you have graded the assignments, have a writing conference with the students. (This unit schedules one in Lesson Twenty.) After the writing conference, allow students to revise their papers using your suggestions and corrections. Give them about three days from the date they receive their papers to complete the revision. I suggest grading the revisions on an A-C-E scale (all revisions well-done, some revisions made, few or no revisions made). This will speed your grading time and still give some credit for the students' efforts.

WRITING ASSIGNMENT #2 - *Romeo and Juliet*

PROMPT
Your assignment is to write a complete composition about the background information you researched at the beginning of this unit.

PREWRITING
Start by looking at the notes you took as you were gathering information. Then, look at the fact sheet you and the members of your group compiled. Think of one statement you could make about all this information. That will be the main idea of your paper. Can the information you have gathered be put into categories? (Are there some things that naturally go together?) Is there a logical progression of ideas? (Can your information be put in chronological order? If so, do it.)

DRAFTING
First write a paragraph in which you introduce the topic of your composition. The paragraphs in the body of your composition will all support or explain your main topic. The paragraphs should flow from idea to idea (from category to category, or in chronological order from earliest to latest, etc.). Your final paragraph should include the conclusions you can draw from the information presented and should bring your composition to a close.

PROMPT
When you finish the rough draft of your paper, ask a student who sits near you to read it. After reading your rough draft, he/she should tell you what he/she liked best about your work, which parts were difficult to understand, and ways in which your work could be improved. Reread your paper considering your critic's comments, and make the corrections you think are necessary.

PROOFREADING
Do a final proofreading of your paper double-checking your grammar, spelling, organization, and the clarity of your ideas.

LESSON SIXTEEN

<u>Objectives</u>
1. To study the play more closely through all five acts
2. To give students the opportunity to practice their personal interaction skills in a small group setting
3. To give students the opportunity to practice their public speaking skills as they report their small group findings

<u>Activity #1</u>
Divide the class into eight groups. Each group should be assigned one of the following topics:
1. Puns/verbal plays on words/humor
2. Age/youth theme
3. Views of love
4. Tragedy of fate
5. Supernatural/dreams
6. "Language of love" (examples of use of language to express emotion)
7. Use of the minor characters

Each group should look at its topic through the entire play, and prepare to "teach" that topic to the class. Group members should divide the work into acts, giving each person of the group a specific act to research. After each member has had time to complete his research, the group members should share their findings with each other. They should then have a small discussion to try to draw any reasonable conclusions they can from the data they collected. One group member should be designated "secretary" to jot down the group's ideas. Another should be designated "spokesperson" to report the group's ideas to the class.

<u>Activity #2</u>
The groups will each report their findings and conclusions to the whole class. The teacher or a student should write down on the board or overhead all of the findings and conclusions. Students should all take notes from the board for later study.

LESSON SEVENTEEN

<u>Objective</u>
To complete the reports begun in Lesson Sixteen.

<u>Activity</u>
Have students complete the reports begun in Lesson Sixteen. Allow ample time for discussion.

LESSON EIGHTEEN

Objectives
    1. To bring some ideas from *Romeo and Juliet* to the present day
    2. To offer practical, professional advice about dealing with tragedy

NOTE: BE SURE TO MAKE ARRANGEMENTS TO HAVE A GUEST SPEAKER FOR TODAY.
    The speaker should be qualified to discuss ways to deal with emotional tragedies. A psychologist or some other person trained in this field. (Someone from a crisis center, hot-line, or similar group might be qualified.)

Activity #1
    Explain to students that they have (in the Extra Discussion Questions) come up with a literary definition of tragedy. Ask them what tragedy is in our world today? What things are tragic? (Get some examples from your students.) Offer several local newspaper headlines about tragic events from your neighborhoods.
    Ask students, "How would you feel in [x] situation." (Note a situation a student has offered or one from the newspaper headlines.)
    Introduce the idea that dealing emotionally with tragedy is difficult at best (look at how Romeo and Juliet handled it, for example. They were so overcome with grief that they committed suicide.) Offer the idea that although suicide is an option, it is not the best option.

Activity #2
    Introduce your guest speaker who will make a presentation and talk with your class about tragedy, grief, death and ways to deal with our emotional upsets. Turn the remainder of this class period over to your speaker.

LESSON NINETEEN

Objectives
    1. To give students the opportunity to practice writing to persuade
    2. To give the teacher a chance to evaluate students' individual writing
    3. To give students the opportunity to correct their writing errors and produce an error-free paper
    4. To give students the opportunity to review and put into practice information the speaker presented in Lesson Eighteen.

Activity
    Distribute Writing Assignment 3. Discuss the directions in detail and give students ample time to complete the assignment.

WRITING ASSIGNMENT #3 - *Romeo and Juliet*

PROMPT

We have discussed that *Romeo and Juliet* is a tragedy, and you have heard the advice of a professional regarding ways to deal with emotional tragedies. You are there beside Juliet at the moment she is about to end her life. Your assignment is to persuade Juliet not to commit suicide.

PREWRITING

Stop and think for a minute. Your friend, Juliet, has just discovered that her boyfriend/husband, Romeo, has just killed himself. He is dead. How does Juliet feel? What could you possibly say that would make any difference to her at this moment of crisis in her life? Jot down your ideas. Consider the things you discussed in your last class period about ways to deal with tragedy. Jot down the things you think are most important to remember, especially in Juliet's case.

DRAFTING

Bearing all the things you considered in the Prewriting stage in mind, write out what you would say and do to persuade Juliet not to commit suicide.

PROMPT

When you finish the rough draft of your paper, ask a student who sits near you to read it. After reading your rough draft, he/she should tell you what he/she liked best about your work, which parts were difficult to understand, and ways in which your work could be improved. Reread your paper considering your critic's comments, and make the corrections you think are necessary.

PROOFREADING

Do a final proofreading of your paper double-checking your grammar, spelling, organization, and the clarity of your ideas.

LESSON TWENTY

Objectives
    1. To review the main ideas presented in *Romeo and Juliet*
    2. To give students personal feedback about their writing

Activity #1

    Choose one of the review games/activities included in the packet and spend your class period as outlined there. Some materials for these activities are located in the Extra Activities Packet section of this unit.

    While students are doing their review activities, call individuals to your desk (or some other private area) to discuss their papers from Writing Assignment 2. A Writing Evaluation Form is included with this unit to help structure your conferences.

Activity #2

    Remind students that the Unit Test will be in the next class meeting. Stress the review of the Study Guides and their class notes as a last minute, brush-up review for homework.

WRITING EVALUATION FORM - *Romeo and Juliet*

Name _____ Date _____

Writing Assignment #1 for the *Romeo and Juliet* unit   Grade _____

Circle One For Each Item:

Grammar: correct   errors noted on paper

Spelling: correct   errors noted on paper

Punctuation: correct   errors noted on paper

Legibility: excellent   good   fair   poor

Strengths:

Weaknesses:

Comments/Suggestions:

REVIEW GAMES/ACTIVITIES - *Romeo and Juliet*

1. Ask the class to make up a unit test for Romeo and Juliet. The test should have 4 sections: matching, true/false, short answer, and essay. Students may use 1/2 period to make the test and then swap papers and use the other 1/2 class period to take a test a classmate has devised. (open book) You may want to use the unit test included in this packet or take questions from the students' unit tests to formulate your own test.

2. Take 1/2 period for students to make up true and false questions (including the answers). Collect the papers and divide the class into two teams. Draw a big tic-tac-toe board on the chalk board. Make one team X and one team O. Ask questions to each side, giving each student one turn. If the question is answered correctly, that students' team's letter (X or O) is placed in the box. If the answer is incorrect, no mark is placed in the box. The object is to get three marks in a row like tic-tac-toe. You may want to keep track of the number of games won for each team.

3. Take 1/2 period for students to make up questions (true/false and short answer). Collect the questions. Divide the class into two teams. You'll alternate asking questions to individual members of teams A & B (like in a spelling bee). The question keeps going from A to B until it is correctly answered, then a new question is asked. A correct answer does not allow the team to get another question. Correct answers are +2 points; incorrect answers are -1 point.

4. Have students pair up and quiz each other from their study guides and class notes.

5. Give students a *Romeo and Juliet* crossword puzzle to complete.

6. Divide your class into two teams. Use the *Romeo and Juliet* crossword words with their letters jumbled as a word list. Student 1 from Team A faces off against Student 1 from Team B. You write the first jumbled word on the board. The first student (1A or 1B) to unscramble the word wins the chance for his/her team to score points. If 1A wins the jumble, go to student 2A and give him/her a clue. He/she must give you the correct word which matches that clue. If he/she does, Team A scores a point, and you give student 3A a clue for which you expect another correct response. Continue giving Team A clues until some team member makes an incorrect response. An incorrect response sends the game back to the jumbled-word face off, this time with students 2A and 2B. Instead of repeating giving clues to the first few students of each team, continue with the student after the one who gave the last incorrect response on the team. For example, if Team B wins the jumbled-word face-off, and student 5B gave the last incorrect answer for Team B, you would start this round of clue questions with student 6B, and so on. The team with the most points wins!

UNIT TESTS

Thi page is left blank for two-sided printing.

SHORT ANSWER UNIT TEST 1 - *Romeo and Juliet*

I. Matching/Identify

___ 1. Benvolio   A. He kills himself when he thinks Juliet is dead

___ 2. Capulet   B. Romeo kills him to avenge his friend's death

___ 3. Friar Laurence   C. He gives a feast to introduce Juliet to bachelors

___ 4. Juliet   D. He is slain by Tybalt

___ 5. Lady Capulet   E. Capulet's favored suitor for Juliet

___ 6. Lady Montague   F. He agrees to marry Romeo and Juliet

___ 7. Mercutio   G. He explains the circumstances of Tybalt's death

___ 8. Montague   H. She dies grieving for her son, Romeo

___ 9. Nurse   I. She refused Romeo's love and caused his depression

___ 10. Paris   J. Juliet's servant and mentor

___ 11. Prince   K. Both Paris and Romeo want to marry her

___ 12. Romeo   L. Romeo's father

___ 13. Rosaline   M. She wants the Prince to execute Romeo

___ 14. Tybalt   N. He sends Romeo into exile

Romeo Short Answer Unit Test 1 Page 2

II. Short Answer

1. Why do Sampson and Gregory fight with Montague's men?

2. Why is Romeo so sad in the beginning of the play?

3. How do Romeo and Juliet meet?

4. Why does Friar Laurence agree to marry Romeo and Juliet?

5. How does Mercutio die?

6. How did Romeo's killing Tybalt put Juliet in a bad position?

7. What plans did Juliet and Friar Laurence make? (Be specific.)

8. What are the circumstances of Paris' death?

9. After she wakes up from being drugged, why does Juliet kill herself?

10. Why does the Prince say "All are punished"?

Romeo Short Answer Unit Test 1 Page 3

III. Explain the significance of the following quotations:

1. Oh, dear account! My life is my foe's debt. (Romeo)

2. That which we call a rose/ By any other name would smell as sweet. (Juliet)

3. In one respect I'll thy assistant be;/ For this alliance may so happy prove,/ To turn your households' rancor to pure love. (Friar)

4. Affliction is enamored of thy parts,/ And thou art wedded to calamity. (Friar)

5. Death is my son-in-law. Death is my heir (Capulet)

Romeo Short Answer Unit Test 1 Page 4

IV. Vocabulary

Listen to the vocabulary words and write them down.
Go back and write in the correct definition next to each word.

1.

2.

3.

4.

5.

6.

7.

8.

9.

10.

SHORT ANSWER UNIT TEST 2 - *Romeo and Juliet*

I. Matching

___ 1. Benvolio   A. He agrees to marry Romeo and Juliet

___ 2. Capulet   B. He sends Romeo into exile

___ 3. Friar Laurence   C. She dies grieving for her son, Romeo

___ 4. Juliet   D. Romeo's father

___ 5. Lady Capulet   E. She refused Romeo's love and caused his depression

___ 6. Lady Montague   F. He kills himself when he thinks Juliet is dead

___ 7. Mercutio   G. He gives a feast to introduce Juliet to bachelors

___ 8. Montague   H. He explains the circumstances of Tybalt's death

___ 9. Nurse   I. Capulet's favored suitor for Juliet

___ 10. Paris   J. Both Paris and Romeo want to marry her

___ 11. Prince   K. Juliet's servant and mentor

___ 12. Romeo   L. She wants the Prince to execute Romeo

___ 13. Rosaline   M. He is slain by Tybalt

___ 14. Tybalt   N. Romeo kills him to avenge his friend's death

Romeo Short Answer Unit Test 2 Page 2

II. Short Answer

1. When Montague and Capulet enter and see the disturbance, they want to fight, too. What do their wives say?

2. What does Romeo mean when he says, "Oh, dear account! My life is my foe's debt"?

3. Why does Friar Laurence agree to marry Romeo and Juliet?

4. In Act III, Mercutio and Benvolio get into a conflict with Tybalt. What does Romeo do when he comes upon them? Why?

5. Why did Romeo's killing Tybalt put Juliet in a bad position? What did she finally decide?

6. What plans do Friar Laurence and Juliet make?

7. What went wrong with the Friar's plan?

8. What are the circumstances of Paris' death?

Romeo Short Answer Unit Test 2 Page 3

III. Composition

Explain in detail the significance of the last lines of the play explaining all the possible ways it is true:

"For never was a story of more woe
Than this of Juliet and her Romeo."

Romeo Short Answer Unit Test 2 Page 4

IV. Vocabulary
    Listen to the vocabulary words and write them down.
    Go back and write in the correct definitions next to the words.

1.

2.

3.

4.

5.

6.

7.

8.

9.

10.

KEY: SHORT ANSWER UNIT TESTS - *Romeo and Juliet*

The short answer questions are taken directly from the study guides. If you need to look up the answers, you will find them in the study guide section.

Answers to the composition questions will vary depending on your class discussions and the level of your students.

For the vocabulary section of the test, choose ten of the words from the vocabulary lists to read orally for your students.

The answers to the matching section of the test are below.

Answers to the matching section of the Advanced Short Answer Unit Test are the same as for Short Answer Unit Test #2.

Test #1	Test #2
1. G	1. H
2. C	2. G
3. F	3. A
4. K	4. J
5. M	5. L
6. H	6. C
7. D	7. M
8. L	8. D
9. J	9. K
10. E	10. I
11. N	11. B
12. A	12. F
13. I	13. E
14. B	14. N

ADVANCED SHORT ANSWER UNIT TEST - *Romeo and Juliet*

I. Matching

___ 1. Benvolio   A. He agrees to marry Romeo and Juliet

___ 2. Capulet   B. He sends Romeo into exile

___ 3. Friar Laurence   C. She dies grieving for her son, Romeo

___ 4. Juliet   D. Romeo's father

___ 5. Lady Capulet   E. She refused Romeo's love and caused his depression

___ 6. Lady Montague   F. He kills himself when he thinks Juliet is dead

___ 7. Mercutio   G. He gives a feast to introduce Juliet to bachelors

___ 8. Montague   H. He explains the circumstances of Tybalt's death

___ 9. Nurse   I. Capulet's favored suitor for Juliet

___ 10. Paris   J. Both Paris and Romeo want to marry her

___ 11. Prince   K. Juliet's servant and mentor

___ 12. Romeo   L. She wants the Prince to execute Romeo

___ 13. Rosaline   M. He is slain by Tybalt

___ 14. Tybalt   N. Romeo kills him to avenge his friend's death

Romeo Advanced Short Answer Unit Test Page 2

II. Short Answer

1. Where is the climax of the play? Explain your choice.

2. Define "tragedy" in the theatrical/literary sense of the word. Explain why *Romeo and Juliet* is a tragedy.

3. What things in *Romeo and Juliet* are due to fate, and what effect does that have on our perception of the play?

4. Who is responsible for Romeo's death? Explain your answer.

5. When and how are the supernatural and/or dreams used in the play?

6. Give at least three examples of the age/youth theme in *Romeo and Juliet*.

7. Explain why *Romeo and Juliet* has stood the test of time and is still being read and performed today.

Romeo Advanced Short Answer Unit Test Page 3

III. Quotations: Explain the significance of the following quotations:

1. What, drawn, and talk of peace! I hate the word
   As I hate Hell, all Montagues, and thee. (I.i,77-78)

2. That which we call a rose
   By any other name would smell as sweet. (II.ii,43-44)

3. In one respect I'll thy assistant be;
   For this alliance may so happy prove,
   To turn your households' rancor to pure love. (II.iii,90-93)

4. Death is my son-in-law, Death is my heir (IV.v,38)

5. Capulet! Montague!
   See what a scourge is laid upon your hate
   That Heaven finds means to kill your joys with love!
   And I, for winking at your discords too,
   Have lost a brace of kinsmen. All are punished. (V.iii,291-295)

Romeo Advanced Short Answer Unit Test Page 4

IV. Vocabulary

Listen and write down the vocabulary words. Go back and write a composition using all of the vocabulary words. The composition must relate in some way to *Romeo and Juliet*.

MULTIPLE CHOICE UNIT TEST 1 - *Romeo and Juliet*

I. Matching

___ 1. Benvolio   A. He kills himself when he thinks Juliet is dead

___ 2. Capulet   B. Romeo kills him to avenge his friend's death

___ 3. Friar Laurence   C. He gives a feast to introduce Juliet to bachelors

___ 4. Juliet   D. He is slain by Tybalt

___ 5. Lady Capulet   E. Capulet's favored suitor for Juliet

___ 6. Lady Montague   F. He agrees to marry Romeo and Juliet

___ 7. Mercutio   G. He explains the circumstances of Tybalt's death

___ 8. Montague   H. She dies grieving for her son, Romeo

___ 9. Nurse   I. She refused Romeo's love and caused his depression

___ 10. Paris   J. Juliet's servant and mentor

___ 11. Prince   K. Both Paris and Romeo want to marry her

___ 12. Romeo   L. Romeo's father

___ 13. Rosaline   M. She wants the Prince to execute Romeo

___ 14. Tybalt   N. He sends Romeo into exile

Romeo Multiple Choice Test 1 Page 2

II. Multiple Choice

1. Why is Romeo so sad?
    a. He wanted to fight, but he missed it.
    b. The girl he loves does not want to get married.
    c. He had an argument with his cousin Benvolio.
    d. He just lost his best friend.

2. What does Romeo mean when he says, "Oh, dear account! My life is my foe's debt"?
    a. Although the dinner was expensive, he didn't enjoy it.
    b. He is glad that Tybalt left the banquet without fighting.
    c. His love for Juliet has brought him out of his depression. Since she is a Capulet, he owes his enemy for his new happiness.
    d. He went to the party to get a glimpse of Rosaline. When he saw Rosaline dancing with another young man, he felt jealous and angry.

3. Why does Friar Laurence agree to marry Romeo and Juliet?
    a. Romeo offers him a lot of money.
    b. He doesn't like Paris, and doesn't think Juliet should marry him.
    c. He is obliged by the laws of the church to marry anyone who asks him.
    d. He hopes that it will help to end the feud between the families.

4. What punishment did the Prince give Romeo for fighting?
    a. Death
    b. Exile
    c. Twenty years in jail
    d. A fine of 5,000 lira

5. Romeo's slaying of Tybalt put Juliet in an awkward position. What did she decide to do?
    a. To weep for Romeo's banishment
    b. To weep for both Romeo and Tybalt
    c. To weep for Tybalt's death
    d. Not to weep for either of them

6. What plans do Friar Laurence and Juliet make?
    a. They will tell Capulet the truth and ask him to beg the Prince to allow Romeo's return.
    b. Juliet should agree to marry Paris. On the eve of her wedding, she should drink a potion that will make her appear dead. After it wears off, she should go to Mantua to be with Romeo.
    c. She should threaten to kill herself if her father makes her marry Paris.
    d. The Nurse will help her disguise herself and run away that very night. They will go to another town. Friar Laurence will send Romeo there in a week.

Romeo Multiple Choice Test 1 Page 3

7. What news does Balthasar bring Romeo? How does Romeo react?
   a. Balthasar tells Romeo where to meet Juliet and the Nurse. Romeo happily gets ready to leave.
   b. Balthasar tells Romeo that Juliet has married Paris. Romeo swears to return and kill Paris.
   c. Balthasar tells Romeo of Juliet's death. Romeo rushes out to the apothecary to get poison. He goes to Juliet's grave to drink the poison.
   d. Balthasar tells Romeo what Friar Lawrence has arranged with the Prince. Romeo is free to return to be with Juliet.

8. What went wrong with the Friar's plan?
   a. The Prince changed his mind about the pardon.
   b. The potion was too strong and killed Juliet.
   c. The nurse would not cooperate.
   d. His letter never got to Romeo, so Romeo didn't know that Juliet was not really dead.

9. What are the circumstances of Paris's death?
   a. Capulet is angry that Juliet killed herself. He blames Paris, and kills him.
   b. Paris and Romeo meet at Juliet's tomb. Paris starts a fight, and Romeo kills him.
   c. Paris finds the remains of the potion that Juliet took. He swallows it and kills himself.
   d. Paris kills Romeo, and the Prince orders him to be killed.

10. After she wakes up from being drugged, why does Juliet kill herself with Romeo's dagger?
    a. She sees Romeo dead from the poison. Since there is no poison left, she kills herself with his dagger.
    b. She realizes how foolish she had been, and she is afraid to be discovered by her father.
    c. She is still dazed by the potion. She picks up the knife and then trips, accidently killing herself.
    d. She is afraid the Prince will think she killed Romeo intentionally, and either banish her or put her to death.

11. Why does Romeo decide to go to the feast even though he is not invited?
    a. Rosaline, the girl he loves, will be there.
    b. He wants to make peace with the Capulets.
    c. Benvolio offers to introduce him to Juliet.
    d. His favorite foods are going to be served.

12. How do Mercutio and Tybalt die?
    a. Romeo kills them both.
    b. Benvolio kills Mercutio, and Romeo kills Tybalt.
    c. Tybalt kills Mercutio, and Romeo kills Tybalt.
    d. Mercutio and Tybalt kill each other

Romeo Multiple Choice Test 1 Page 4

III. Quotations: Identify the speaker.

    A=Romeo   B=Juliet   C=Friar Laurence   D= Capulet

    E. Montague   F= Prince   G=Lady Montague   H=Lady Capulet

1. Oh, dear account! My life is my foe's debt.

2. That which we call a rose/ By any other name would smell as sweet.

3. In one respect I'll thy assistant be;/ For this alliance may so happy prove,/ To turn your households' rancor to pure love.

4. Affliction is enamored of thy parts,/ And thou art wedded to calamity.

5. Death is my son-in-law. Death is my heir

6. If ever you disturb our streets again,/Your lives shall pay the forfeit of peace.

7. Parting is such sweet sorrow.

8. Oh, I am fortune's fool!

9. Graze where you will, you shall not house with me.

10. A crutch, a crutch! Why call you for a sword?

Romeo Multiple Choice Test 1 Page 5

IV. Vocabulary

___ 1. BODES   A. to be an omen of

___ 2. POSTERITY   B. to gather; collect

___ 3. PURGED   C. a church office endowed with fixed capital assets

___ 4. LANGUISH   D. a prayer

___ 5. RANCOR   E. to express grief for or about

___ 6. PENURY   F. rough and stormy

___ 7. BOISTEROUS   G. a person who holds controversial opinions

___ 8. DISCOURSE   H. destitution

___ 9. LAMENTABLE   I. to free from impurities

___ 10. BESEECH   J. well grounded

___ 11. LOATHED   K. to belong as a proper function or part

___ 12. VALIDITY   L. to narrate or discuss

___ 13. HERETICS   M. a cloak

___ 14. ESTEEM   N. future generations

___ 15. APPERTAINING O. bitter

___ 16. IMPUTE   P. to attribute; credit

___ 17. MANTLE   Q. regard with respect

___ 18. BENEFICE   R. to dislike

___ 19. CULLED   S. to be or become weak or feeble

___ 20. ORISONS   T. to request earnestly

MULTIPLE CHOICE UNIT TEST 2 - *Romeo and Juliet*

I. Matching

___ 1. Benvolio   A. He agrees to marry Romeo and Juliet

___ 2. Capulet   B. He sends Romeo into exile

___ 3. Friar Laurence   C. She dies grieving for her son, Romeo

___ 4. Juliet   D. Romeo's father

___ 5. Lady Capulet   E. She refused Romeo's love and caused his depression

___ 6. Lady Montague   F. He kills himself when he thinks Juliet is dead

___ 7. Mercutio   G. He gives a feast to introduce Juliet to bachelors

___ 8. Montague   H. He explains the circumstances of Tybalt's death

___ 9. Nurse   I. Capulet's favored suitor for Juliet

___ 10. Paris   J. Both Paris and Romeo want to marry her

___ 11. Prince   K. Juliet's servant and mentor

___ 12. Romeo   L. She wants the Prince to execute Romeo

___ 13. Rosaline   M. He is slain by Tybalt

___ 14. Tybalt   N. Romeo kills him to avenge his friend's death

Romeo Multiple Choice Test 2 Page 2

II. Multiple Choice
1. Why is Romeo so sad?
	a. He wanted to fight, but he missed it.
	b. He just lost his best friend.
	c. He had an argument with his cousin Benvolio.
	d. The girl he loves does not want to get married.

2. What does Romeo mean when he says, "Oh, dear account! My life is my foe's debt"?
	a. Although the dinner was expensive, he didn't enjoy it.
	b. His love for Juliet has brought him out of his depression. Since she is a Capulet, he owes his enemy for his new happiness.
	c. He is glad that Tybalt left the banquet without fighting.
	d. He went to the party to get a glimpse of Rosaline. When he saw Rosaline dancing with another young man, he felt jealous and angry.

3. Why does Friar Laurence agree to marry Romeo and Juliet?
	a. He hopes that it will help to end the feud between the families.
	b. He doesn't like Paris, and doesn't think Juliet should marry him.
	c. He is obliged by the laws of the church to marry anyone who asks him.
	d. Romeo offers him a lot of money.

4. What punishment did the Prince give Romeo for fighting?
	a. Death
	b. Twenty years in jail
	c. Exile
	d. A fine of 5,000 lira

5. Romeo's killing Tybalt put Juliet in a bad position. What did she finally decide?
	a. Not to weep for either of them
	b. To weep for both Romeo and Tybalt
	c. To weep only for Tybalt
	d. To weep only for Romeo's banishment

6. What plans do Friar Laurence and Juliet make?
	a. They will tell Capulet the truth and ask him to beg the Prince to allow Romeo's return.
	b. She should threaten to kill herself if her father makes her marry Paris.
	c. Juliet should agree to marry Paris. On the eve of her wedding, she should drink a potion that will make her appear dead. After it wears off, she should go to Mantua to be with Romeo.
	d. The Nurse will help her disguise herself and run away that very night. They will go to another town. Friar Laurence will send Romeo there in a week.

Romeo Multiple Choice Test 2 Page 3

7. What news does Balthasar bring Romeo? How does Romeo react?
   a. Balthasar tells Romeo of Juliet's death. Romeo rushes out to the apothecary to get poison. He goes to Juliet's grave to drink the poison.
   b. Balthasar tells Romeo that Juliet has married Paris. Romeo swears to return and kill Paris.
   c. Balthasar tells Romeo where to meet Juliet and the Nurse. Romeo happily gets ready to leave.
   d. Balthasar tells Romeo what Friar Lawrence has arranged with the Prince. Romeo is free to return to be with Juliet.

8. What went wrong with the Friar's plan?
   a. The Prince changed his mind about the pardon.
   b. His letter never got to Romeo, so Romeo didn't know that Juliet was not really dead.
   c. The nurse would not cooperate.
   d. The potion was too strong and killed Juliet.

9. What are the circumstances of Paris' death?
   a. Capulet is angry that Juliet killed herself. He blames Paris, and kills him.
   b. Paris kills Romeo, and the Prince orders him to be killed.
   c. Paris finds the remains of the potion that Juliet took. He swallows it and kills himself.
   d. Paris and Romeo meet at Juliet's tomb. Paris starts a fight, and Romeo kills him.

10. After she wakes up from being drugged, why does Juliet kill herself with Romeo's dagger?
    a. She realizes how foolish she had been, and she is afraid to be discovered by her father.
    b. She sees Romeo dead from the poison. Since there is no poison left, she kills herself with his dagger.
    c. She is still dazed by the potion. She picks up the knife and then trips, accidently killing herself.
    d. She is afraid the Prince will think she killed Romeo intentionally, and either banish her or put her to death.

11. Why does Romeo decide to go to the feast even though he is not invited?
    a. Benvolio offers to introduce him to Juliet.
    b. He wants to make peace with the Capulets.
    c. Rosaline, the girl he loves, will be there.
    d. His favorite foods are going to be served.

12. How do Mercutio and Tybalt die?
    a. Tybalt kills Mercutio, and Romeo kills Tybalt.
    b. Benvolio kills Mercutio, and Romeo kills Tybalt.
    c. Romeo kills them both.
    d. Mercutio and Tybalt kill each other

Romeo Multiple Choice Test 2 Page 4

III. Quotations: Identify the speaker.

    A=Friar Laurence   B=Romeo   C=Juliet   D= Prince

    E. Capulet   F= Montague   G=Lady Capulet   H=Lady Montague

1. Oh, dear account! My life is my foe's debt.

2. That which we call a rose/ By any other name would smell as sweet.

3. In one respect I'll thy assistant be;/ For this alliance may so happy prove,/ To turn your households' rancor to pure love.

4. Affliction is enamored of thy parts,/ And thou art wedded to calamity.

5. Death is my son-in-law. Death is my heir

6. If ever you disturb our streets again,/Your lives shall pay the forfeit of peace.

7. Parting is such sweet sorrow.

8. Oh, I am fortune's fool!

9. Graze where you will, you shall not house with me.

10. A crutch, a crutch! Why call you for a sword?

Romeo Multiple Choice Test 2 Page 5 IV. Vocabulary

___	1. INUNDATION	A. to be or become weak or feeble
___	2. ORISONS	B. a funeral hymn or lament
___	3. BOISTEROUS	C. rough and stormy
___	4. BEGUILED	D. a person who holds controversial opinions
___	5. LANGUISH	E. to make (something already developed) greater
___	6. PURGED	F. a prayer
___	7. DIRGES	G. a violation of the law
___	8. POSTERITY	H. to belong as proper function or part
___	9. CONSORT	I. destitution
___	10. CHIDE	J. a companion or partner
___	11. APPERTAINING	K. evil; wicked
___	12. ABHORS	L. a cloak
___	13. HERETICS	M. to express disapproval
___	14. PENURY	N. to reject vehemently
___	15. PRESAGE	O. an omen
___	16. PERNICIOUS	P. future generations
___	17. AUGMENTING	Q. to deceive by guile
___	18. MANTLE	R. to submit to settlement or judgment by arbitration
___	19. ARBITRATING	S. to cover with water
___	20. TRANSGRESSION	T. to free from impurities

ANSWER SHEET - *Romeo and Juliet*
Multiple Choice Unit Tests

I. Matching	II. Multiple Choice	III. Quotes	IV. Vocabulary
1. ___	1. ___	1. ___	1. ___
2. ___	2. ___	2. ___	2. ___
3. ___	3. ___	3. ___	3. ___
4. ___	4. ___	4. ___	4. ___
5. ___	5. ___	5. ___	5. ___
6. ___	6. ___	6. ___	6. ___
7. ___	7. ___	7. ___	7. ___
8. ___	8. ___	8. ___	8. ___
9. ___	9. ___	9. ___	9. ___
10. ___	10. ___	10. ___	10. ___
11. ___	11. ___		11. ___
12. ___	12. ___		12. ___
13. ___			13. ___
14. ___			14. ___
			15. ___
			16. ___
			17. ___
			18. ___
			19. ___
			20. ___

ANSWER KEY MULTIPLE CHOICE UNIT TESTS – *Romeo and Juliet*

Answers to Unit Test 1 are in the left column. Answers to Unit Test 2 are in the right column.

I. Matching	II. Multiple Choice	III. Quotes	IV. Vocabulary
1. G H	1. B D	1. A B	1. A S
2. C G	2. C B	2. B C	2. N F
3. F A	3. D A	3. C A	3. I C
4. K J	4. B C	4. C A	4. S Q
5. M L	5. A D	5. D E	5. O A
6. H C	6. B C	6. F D	6. H T
7. D M	7. C A	7. B C	7. F B
8. L D	8. D B	8. A B	8. L P
9. J K	9. B D	9. D E	9. E J
10. E I	10. A B	10. H G	10. T M
11. N B	11. A C		11. R H
12. A F	12. C A		12. J N
13. I E			13. G D
14. B N			14. Q I
			15. K O
			16. P K
			17. M E
			18. C L
			19. B R
			20. D G

Thi page is left blank for two-sided printing.

UNIT RESOURCE MATERIALS

Thi page is left blank for two-sided printing.

BULLETIN BOARD IDEAS - *Romeo and Juliet*

1. Save one corner of the board for the best of students' *Romeo and Juliet* writing assignments.

2. Post articles of criticism about the play.

3. Post enlarged photos taken of a performance of the play. If none are available, have your students create costumes and present scenes from the play and take their photos for next year's bulletin board.

4. Take one of the word search puzzles from the extra activities packet and with a marker copy it over in a large size on the bulletin board. Write the clue words to find to one side. Invite students prior to and after class to find the words and circle them on the bulletin board.

5. Do a bulletin board about careers in the theater.

6. Do a bulletin board with information about youth crisis hotlines, etc. for people trying to cope with emotional stress.

7. Do a bulletin board about Shakespeare. Post a brief summary of his life next to his picture. All around the bulletin board, post "playbills" for each of his major works with a little summary of the plot of each play written inside.

8. Make a bulletin board about the world's (fact and fiction) great, famous (or infamous) couples. (Romeo and Juliet, Antony and Cleopatra, Ginger Rogers and Fred Astaire, Bonnie and Clyde, etc.)

9. Write several of the most significant quotations from the play onto the board on brightly colored paper.

10. Make a "Dear Abby" bulletin board in conjunction with the introductory activity and Writing Assignment 1.

11. Make a bulletin board listing the vocabulary words for this unit. As you complete sections of the play and discuss the vocabulary for each section, write the definitions on the bulletin board. (If your board is one students face frequently, it will help them learn the words.)

EXTRA ACTIVITIES

One of the difficulties in teaching literature is that all students don't read at the same speed. One student who likes to read may take the book home and finish it in a day or two. Sometimes a few students finish the in-class assignments early. The problem, then, is finding suitable extra activities for students.

The best thing I've found is to keep a little library in the classroom. For this unit on *Romeo and Juliet*, you might check out from the school library other related books and articles about the history of courting practices, the history of the use of drugs and potions, romance in fiction, and critics' articles about *Romeo and Juliet*. Other works by Shakespeare and/or simplified versions of Shakespeare's works would also be good to have in your classroom library.

Other things you may keep on hand are puzzles. We have made some relating directly to *Romeo and Juliet* for you. Feel free to duplicate them.

Some students may like to draw. You might devise a contest or allow some extra-credit grade for students who draw characters or scenes from *Romeo and Juliet*. Note, too, that if the students do not want to keep their drawings you may pick up some extra bulletin board materials this way. If you have a contest and you supply the prize (a CD or something like that perhaps), you could, possibly, make the drawing itself a non-refundable entry fee.

The pages which follow contain games, puzzles and worksheets. The keys, when appropriate, immediately follow the puzzle or worksheet. There are two main groups of activities: one group for the unit; that is, generally relating to the *Romeo and Juliet* text, and another group of activities related strictly to the *Romeo and Juliet* vocabulary.

Directions for these games, puzzles and worksheets are self-explanatory. The object here is to provide you with extra materials you may use in any way you choose.

MORE ACTIVITIES - *Romeo and Juliet*

1. Have students in small groups act out various scenes from the play.

2. Use some of the related topics (noted earlier for an in-class library) as topics for research, reports or written papers, or as topics for guest speakers.

3. Have students act out the final act of the play on your school's stage. Assign parts. Other students should work together to design the actors' costumes and the set. Lines may or may not be memorized (teacher's decision). Perhaps you could present it to another section or two of English classes during your normal class period. (Provide a background narrative for the audience.)

4. Have students design a playbill (front and back and inside flaps) for *Romeo and Juliet*.

5. Have students design a bulletin board (ready to be put up; not just sketched) for *Romeo and Juliet*.

6. Spend time discussing the logic of the plot of *Romeo and Juliet*.

7. After analyzing Shakespeare's writing style, have students experiment imitating his style by rewriting the end of the play.

8. In conjunction with the background information assignment, have an Elizabethan Day. Hold a banquet of Elizabethan food & drink, have students dress in Elizabethan costume, and discuss the politics of the period.

9. Choose a passage from *Romeo and Juliet* (at least 10 lines). Analyze the meter, rhyme and imagery in relationship to the meaning and action of the passage. After doing one together in class, have each student choose one passage to do on his/her own.

10. Have students write a poem or song lyrics about *Romeo and Juliet*.

11. Talk about family feuds. Discuss ways in which families are torn apart (Juliet's decision to marry Romeo, for example), and the effects that are felt by each family member. Discuss ways to help mend family relationships.

12. Have students explain ways *Romeo and Juliet* could be considered a modern story.

13. Show the film *West Side Story*. Compare it to *Romeo and Juliet*.

14. Take time to talk about dreams, the supernatural and the possibility of predicting the future.

WORD SEARCH - *Romeo and Juliet*

```
J B W S C L N E J N K K W S T X W R D Z
Q K E U G A T N O M M E R C U T I O E R
S D R N L T Y O Y X S F A E M P E S A D
P Q A B V H B D M C P P G N F M P A T T
P R E G J O A N R B U L H E O S P L H W
M G P K G E L U F L X A V R Y O W I I K
C T S Y O E T I E A Y U H E I R N N B G
G S E F C C R T O O T R Z S R R D E A F
M P K K H Y N P W R E E O V Z O W S L L
P L A G U E V H S C I N R X W W N Y T L
G Y H R S C X F M H L C V O B F D A H G
J Y S D X N V N Q A U E C Y S A Y K A F
T Q K N J I Q C S R J K J S L E V W S K
H K D Y W R R C F D G R I E V I N G A H
B K W F Q P S A M S O N F X P Z K T R N
```

A _____ o'both your houses. (6)
A _____, a _____! Why call you for your sword? (6)
Act division (5)
Author William (11)
Both Paris and Romeo want to marry her. (6)
He agrees to marry Romeo & Juliet: Friar ___ (8)
He explains the circumstances of Tybalt's death. (8)
He gives a feast to introduce Juliet to bachelors. (7)
He is slain by Tybalt. (8)
He kills himself when he thinks Juliet is dead. (5)
Juliet kills herself with Romeo's (6)
Lady Montague dies ___ for her son, Romeo. (8)
Me thinks I see thee .... as one dead in the bottom of a _____. (4)
My life is my __'s debt. (3)
Paris is a nobleman from this place. (6)
Parting is such sweet _____. (6)

Play division (3)
Predestined future (4)
Romeo climbs over the wall surrounding Capulet's _____. (7)
Romeo drinks it and dies. (6)
Romeo kills him to avenge his friend's death. (6)
Romeo's father (8)
Sends Romeo into exile (6)
Servant of the Capulets (6)
Servant to Romeo (9)
She refused Romeo's love and caused his depression. (8)
She wants the Prince to execute Romeo: ___ Capulet (4)
That which we call a _____ By any other name would smell as sweet. (4)
We are _____, lady, we are _____. (6)
What light through yonder _____ breaks? (6)
_____ is my son-in-law, _____ is my heir. (5)

The numbers indicate the number of letters in the clue word.

WORD SEARCH ANSWER KEY- *Romeo And Juliet*

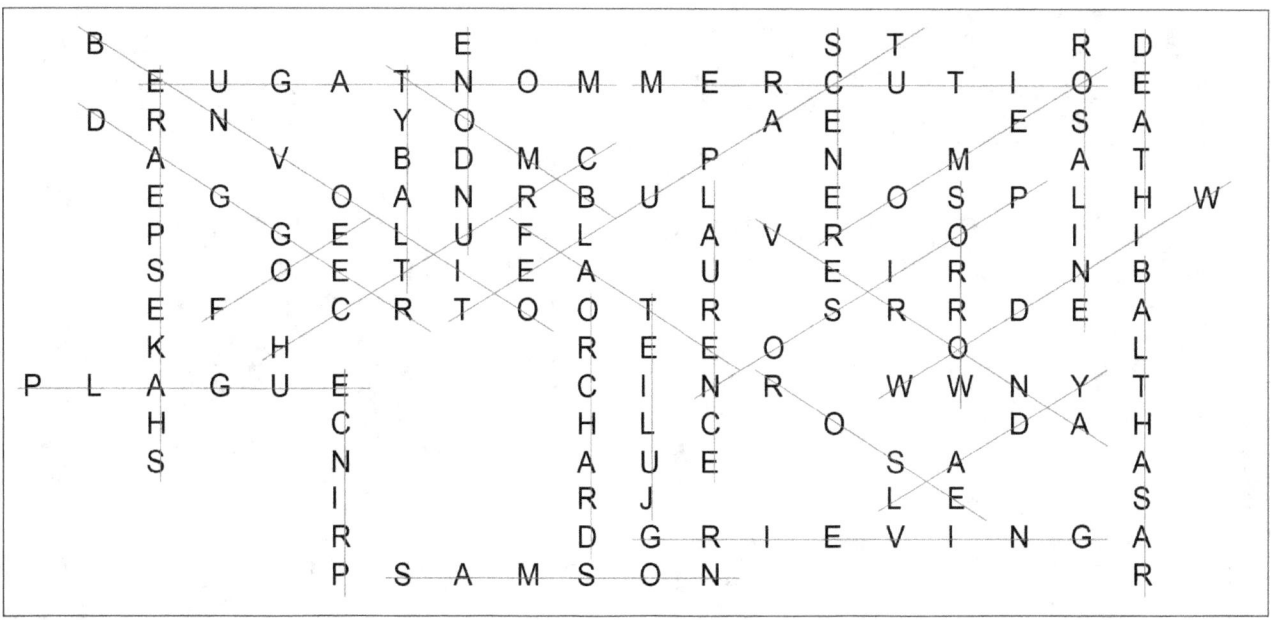

A _____ o'both your houses. (6)
A _____, a _____ ! Why call you for your sword? (6)
Act division (5)
Author William (11)
Both Paris and Romeo want to marry her. (6)
He agrees to marry Romeo & Juliet: Friar ___ (8)
He explains the circumstances of Tybalt's death. (8)
He gives a feast to introduce Juliet to bachelors. (7)
He is slain by Tybalt. (8)
He kills himself when he thinks Juliet is dead. (5)
Juliet kills herself with Romeo's (6)
Lady Montague dies ___ for her son, Romeo. (8)
Me thinks I see thee .... as one dead in the bottom of a _____. (4)
My life is my __'s debt. (3)
Paris is a nobleman from this place. (6)
Parting is such sweet _____. (6)

Play division (3)
Predestined future (4)
Romeo climbs over the wall surrounding Capulet's _____. (7)
Romeo drinks it and dies. (6)
Romeo kills him to avenge his friend's death. (6)
Romeo's father (8)
Sends Romeo into exile (6)
Servant of the Capulets (6)
Servant to Romeo (9)
She refused Romeo's love and caused his depression. (8)
She wants the Prince to execute Romeo: ___ Capulet (4)
That which we call a _____ By any other name would smell as sweet. (4)
We are _____, lady, we are _____. (6)
What light through yonder _____ breaks? (6)
_____ is my son-in-law, _____ is my heir. (5)

105

CROSSWORD PUZZLE - *Romeo and Juliet*

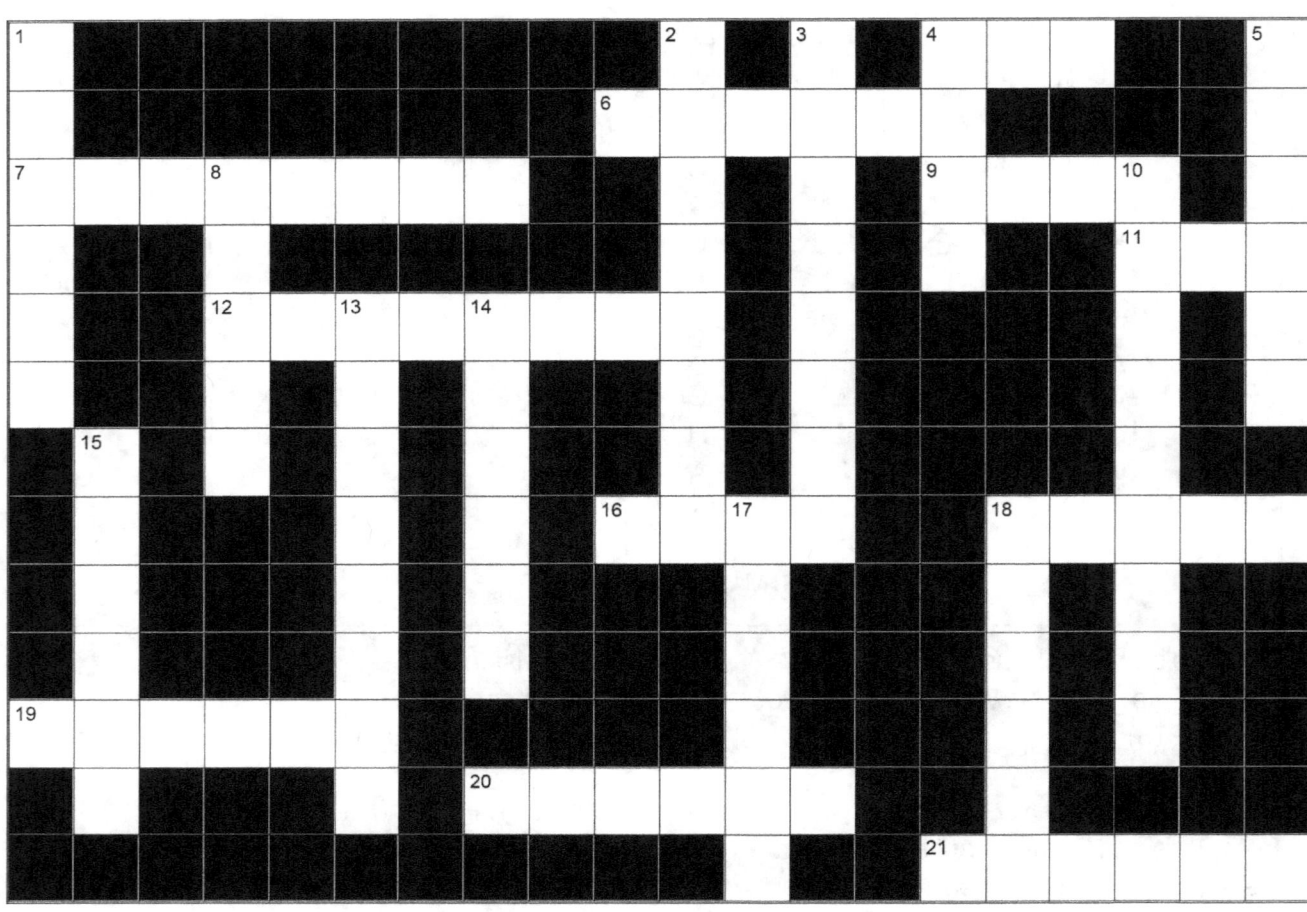

Across
4. My life is my __'s debt.
6. Paris is a nobleman from this place.
7. He agrees to marry Romeo & Juliet: Friar ___
9. Me thinks I see thee .... as one dead in the bottom of a _____.
11. Play division
12. He is slain by Tybalt.
16. That which we call a _____ By any other name would smell as sweet.
18. _____ is my son-in-law, _____ is my heir.
19. Romeo drinks it and dies.
20. What light through yonder _____ breaks?
21. Sends Romeo into exile

Down
1. Both Paris and Romeo want to marry her.
2. He explains the circumstances of Tybalt's death.
3. Romeo's father
4. Predestined future
5. A _____, a _____! Why call you for your sword?
8. He kills himself when he thinks Juliet is dead.
10. Servant to Romeo
13. She refused Romeo's love and caused his depression.
14. We are _____, lady, we are _____.
15. Parting is such sweet _____.
17. Servant of the Capulets
18. Juliet kills herself with Romeo's

CROSSWORD ANSWER KEY - *Romeo and Juliet*

¹J								²		³		⁴F	O	E	⁵
								B		M					C
U							⁶V	E	R	O	N	A			R
⁷L	A	⁸U	R	E	N	C	E			N		⁹T	¹⁰O	M	B
I		O					N			T		E		¹¹A	C	T
E		¹²M	¹³E	¹⁴R	C	U	T	I	O		A			L		C
T			E	O		N		L		G				T		H
	¹⁵S		O	S		D		I		U			H	
	O			A		O		¹⁶R	O	¹⁷S	E		¹⁸D	E	A	T	H
	R			L		N				A			A	S
	R			I		E				M			G	A
¹⁹P	O	I	S	O	N					S			G	R
	W			E		²⁰W	I	N	D	O	W		E
										N		²¹P	R	I	N	C	E

Across
4. My life is my __'s debt.
6. Paris is a nobleman from this place.
7. He agrees to marry Romeo & Juliet: Friar ___
9. Me thinks I see thee .... as one dead in the bottom of a _____.
11. Play division
12. He is slain by Tybalt.
16. That which we call a _____ By any other name would smell as sweet.
18. _____ is my son-in-law, _____ is my heir.
19. Romeo drinks it and dies.
20. What light through yonder _____ breaks?
21. Sends Romeo into exile

Down
1. Both Paris and Romeo want to marry her.
2. He explains the circumstances of Tybalt's death.
3. Romeo's father
4. Predestined future
5. A _____, a _____! Why call you for your sword?
8. He kills himself when he thinks Juliet is dead.
10. Servant to Romeo
13. She refused Romeo's love and caused his depression.
14. We are _____, lady, we are _____.
15. Parting is such sweet _____.
17. Servant of the Capulets
18. Juliet kills herself with Romeo's

MATCHING QUIZ/WORKSHEET 1 - Romeo and Juliet

___ 1. LAURENCE   A. Predestined future

___ 2. TYBALT   B. My life is my ___'s debt.

___ 3. POISON   C. Play division

___ 4. TOMB   D. He gives a feast to introduce Juliet to bachelors.

___ 5. SHAKESPEARE   E. Romeo's father

___ 6. ACT   F. Parting is such sweet _____.

___ 7. ORCHARD   G. Romeo kills him to avenge his friend's death.

___ 8. GRIEVING   H. Author William

___ 9. BALTHASAR   I. He is slain by Tybalt.

___ 10. JULIET   J. A _____, a _____! Why call you for your sword?

___ 11. FOE   K. Servant of the Capulets

___ 12. SAMSON   L. Romeo climbs over the wall surrounding Capulet's _____.

___ 13. MERCUTIO   M. Servant to Romeo

___ 14. MONTAGUE   N. He agrees to marry Romeo & Juliet: Friar ___

___ 15. BENVOLIO   O. Both Paris and Romeo want to marry her.

___ 16. CAPULET   P. We are _____, lady, we are _____.

___ 17. DAGGER   Q. Romeo drinks it and dies.

___ 18. ROSALINE   R. She refused Romeo's love and caused his depression.

___ 19. LADY   S. That which we call a _____ By any other name would smell as sweet.

___ 20. ROSE   T. Act division

___ 21. SCENE   U. He explains the circumstances of Tybalt's death.

___ 22. UNDONE   V. Lady Montague dies ___ for her son, Romeo.

___ 23. CRUTCH   W. Juliet kills herself with Romeo's

___ 24. SORROW   X. Me thinks I see thee .... as one dead in the bottom of a _____.

___ 25. FATE   Y. She wants the Prince to execute Romeo: ___ Capulet

KEY: MATCHING QUIZ/WORKSHEET 1 - Romeo and Juliet

N - 1. LAURENCE		A. Predestined future
G - 2. TYBALT		B. My life is my __'s debt.
Q - 3. POISON		C. Play division
X - 4. TOMB		D. He gives a feast to introduce Juliet to bachelors.
H - 5. SHAKESPEARE		E. Romeo's father
C - 6. ACT		F. Parting is such sweet _____.
L - 7. ORCHARD		G. Romeo kills him to avenge his friend's death.
V - 8. GRIEVING		H. Author William
M - 9. BALTHASAR		I. He is slain by Tybalt.
O - 10. JULIET		J. A _____, a _____! Why call you for your sword?
B - 11. FOE		K. Servant of the Capulets
K - 12. SAMSON		L. Romeo climbs over the wall surrounding Capulet's _____.
I - 13. MERCUTIO		M. Servant to Romeo
E - 14. MONTAGUE		N. He agrees to marry Romeo & Juliet: Friar ___
U - 15. BENVOLIO		O. Both Paris and Romeo want to marry her.
D - 16. CAPULET		P. We are _____, lady, we are _____.
W - 17. DAGGER		Q. Romeo drinks it and dies.
R - 18. ROSALINE		R. She refused Romeo's love and caused his depression.
Y - 19. LADY		S. That which we call a _____ By any other name would smell as sweet.
S - 20. ROSE		T. Act division
T - 21. SCENE		U. He explains the circumstances of Tybalt's death.
P - 22. UNDONE		V. Lady Montague dies ___ for her son, Romeo.
J - 23. CRUTCH		W. Juliet kills herself with Romeo's
F - 24. SORROW		X. Me thinks I see thee .... as one dead in the bottom of a _____.
A - 25. FATE		Y. She wants the Prince to execute Romeo: ___ Capulet

MATCHING QUIZ/WORKSHEET 2 - *Romeo and Juliet*

___ 1. MONTAGUE   A. Servant to Romeo

___ 2. FOE   B. She wants the Prince to execute Romeo: ___ Capulet

___ 3. LADY   C. My life is my __'s debt. ___ 4. PLAGUE   D. Act division

___ 5. ROSALINE   E. A _____, a _____! Why call you for your sword?

___ 6. SCENE   F. Play division

___ 7. BENVOLIO   G. He agrees to marry Romeo & Juliet: Friar ___

___ 8. ORCHARD   H. Lady Montague dies ___ for her son, Romeo.

___ 9. ACT   I. Romeo's father

___ 10. POISON   J. Romeo climbs over the wall surrounding Capulet's _____.

___ 11. DAGGER   K. Me thinks I see thee .... as one dead in the bottom of a _____.

___ 12. FATE   L. Predestined future

___ 13. SHAKESPEARE   M. He explains the circumstances of Tybalt's death.

___ 14. GRIEVING   N. Romeo kills him to avenge his friend's death.

___ 15. CRUTCH   O. Romeo drinks it and dies.

___ 16. TOMB   P. A ____ o'both your houses.

___ 17. LAURENCE   Q. _____ is my son-in-law, _____ is my heir.

___ 18. SORROW   R. Juliet kills herself with Romeo's

___ 19. WINDOW   S. He is slain by Tybalt.

___ 20. VERONA   T. What light through yonder _____ breaks?

___ 21. MERCUTIO   U. Paris is a nobleman from this place.

___ 22. SAMSON   V. She refused Romeo's love and caused his depression.

___ 23. DEATH   W. Author William

___ 24. TYBALT   X. Parting is such sweet _____.

___ 25. BALTHASAR   Y. Servant of the Capulets

KEY: MATCHING QUIZ/WORKSHEET 2 - Romeo and Juliet

I - 1. MONTAGUE		A. Servant to Romeo
C - 2. FOE		B. She wants the Prince to execute Romeo: ___ Capulet
B - 3. LADY		C. My life is my __'s debt.
P - 4. PLAGUE		D. Act division
V - 5. ROSALINE		E. A _____, a _____! Why call you for your sword?
D - 6. SCENE		F. Play division
M - 7. BENVOLIO		G. He agrees to marry Romeo & Juliet: Friar ___
J - 8. ORCHARD		H. Lady Montague dies ___ for her son, Romeo.
F - 9. ACT		I. Romeo's father
O - 10. POISON		J. Romeo climbs over the wall surrounding Capulet's _____.
R - 11. DAGGER		K. Me thinks I see thee .... as one dead in the bottom of a _____.
L - 12. FATE		L. Predestined future
W - 13. SHAKESPEARE		M. He explains the circumstances of Tybalt's death.
H - 14. GRIEVING		N. Romeo kills him to avenge his friend's death.
E - 15. CRUTCH		O. Romeo drinks it and dies.
K - 16. TOMB		P. A ____ o'both your houses.
G - 17. LAURENCE		Q. _____ is my son-in-law, _____ is my heir.
X - 18. SORROW		R. Juliet kills herself with Romeo's
T - 19. WINDOW		S. He is slain by Tybalt.
U - 20. VERONA		T. What light through yonder _____ breaks?
S - 21. MERCUTIO		U. Paris is a nobleman from this place.
Y - 22. SAMSON		V. She refused Romeo's love and caused his depression.
Q - 23. DEATH		W. Author William
N - 24. TYBALT		X. Parting is such sweet _____.
A - 25. BALTHASAR		Y. Servant of the Capulets

JUGGLE LETTER REVIEW GAME CLUE SHEET - *Romeo and Juliet*

SCRAMBLED	WORD	CLUE
APEAUGL	PLAGUE	A _____ o'both your houses
GGEARD	DAGGER	Juliet kills herself with Romeo's
EALAPCLYUTD	LADY CAPULET	She wants the Prince to execute Romeo
ALORNESI	ROSALINE	She refused Romeo's love and caused his depression
ETJULI	JULIET	Both Paris and Romeo want to marry her
LASRTAAHG	BALTHASAR	Servant to Romeo
OOWRRS	SORROW	Parting is such sweet _____.
MROOE	ROMEO	He kills himself when he thinks Juliet is dead
IPSAR	PARIS	Capulet's favored suitor for Juliet
NWDOWI	WINDOW	What light through yonder _____ breaks
RNUES	NURSE	Juliet's servant and mentor
EECSN	SCENE	Act division
TCCHUR	CRUTCH	A _____, a _____! Why call you for your sword?
ATEHD	DEATH	_____ is my son-in-law, _____ is my heir
OVAERN	VERONA	Paris is a nobleman from this place
CTA	ACT	Play division
OENUND	UNDONE	We are _____, lady, we are _____
OEF	FOE	My life is my _____'s debt.
RCOITEUM	MERCUTIO	He is slain by Tybalt
LBOOIVNE	BENVOLIO	He explains the circumstances of Tybalt's death
DOHRRCA	ORCHARD	Romeo climbs over the wall surrounding Capulet's _____.
PTUEACL	CAPULET	He gives a feast to introduce Juliet to bachelors
OPONIS	POISON	Romeo drinks it and dies
EFAT	FATE	Predestined future
RPCENI	PRINCE	Sends Romeo into exile
BMTO	TOMB	Me thinks I see the --- as one dread in the bottom of a _____.
TBLYAT	TYBALT	Romeo kills him to avenge his friend's death

VOCABULARY RESOURCE MATERIALS

Thi page is left blank for two-sided printing.

VOCABULARY WORD SEARCH - *Romeo and Juliet*

```
P E C I T L U O P M P D I R G E B P O Q
R B Y U D W D H E U E V O Q D G E R B T
O E Q V L W F E R H R C Q I A A G E S T
R N G T Z L T G T Y N R H M U S U D C R
O E Z Y E S E A X A I C F P G E I O U A
G F P D E D O D R N C B N E M R L M R N
U I X R I L I G V L I O Y A E P E I E S
E C A L O S C O N S O R T C N A D N D G
T E E B N F C D U R U I I H T L G A K R
U C N X E A A O H S S S D M I D R N B E
P K V Q T S T N U S T O I P N E H T X S
M K I I F T E Y E R D N L Q G R K D K S
I G O Y R U N E P R S S A E N M I T Y I
L N U N W Z V H C L S E V X X A Q Z X O
D N S C I T E R E H Y Y E L T N A M N N
```

A church office endowed with fixed capital assets (8)
A companion or partner (7)
A member of the municipal legislative body (8)
A soft, moist mass of bread, meal or clay (8)
An omen (7)
Bitterness (6)
Challenge the validity of something (7)
Cloak; coat (6)
Comfort in sorrow (6)
Deceived by guile (8)
Deep seated, often mutual hatred (6)
Destitution (6)
Discontinue a session (8)
Disliked (7)
Evil; wicked (10)
Express disapproval (5)
Freed from impurities (6)
Funeral hymn or lament (5)
Gathered; collected (6)
Good health; how sound something is (8)
Incantation used in conjuring (10)
Indistinctly heard; partially hidden from the senses (8)
Jealous (7)
Making something already developed greater (10)
Most common or conspicuous (11)
Moving or progressing very slowly (7)
Narrate or discuss (9)
Person who holds opinions contrary to the beliefs of others in a group (7)
Prayers (7)
Regard with respect (6)
Request earnestly (7)
Those showing irreverence for what is sacred (9)
To attribute; to credit (6)
Violation of a law (13)

The numbers after the clues are the number of letters in the answer.

VOCABULARY WORD SEARCH ANSWER KEY - *Romeo And Juliet*

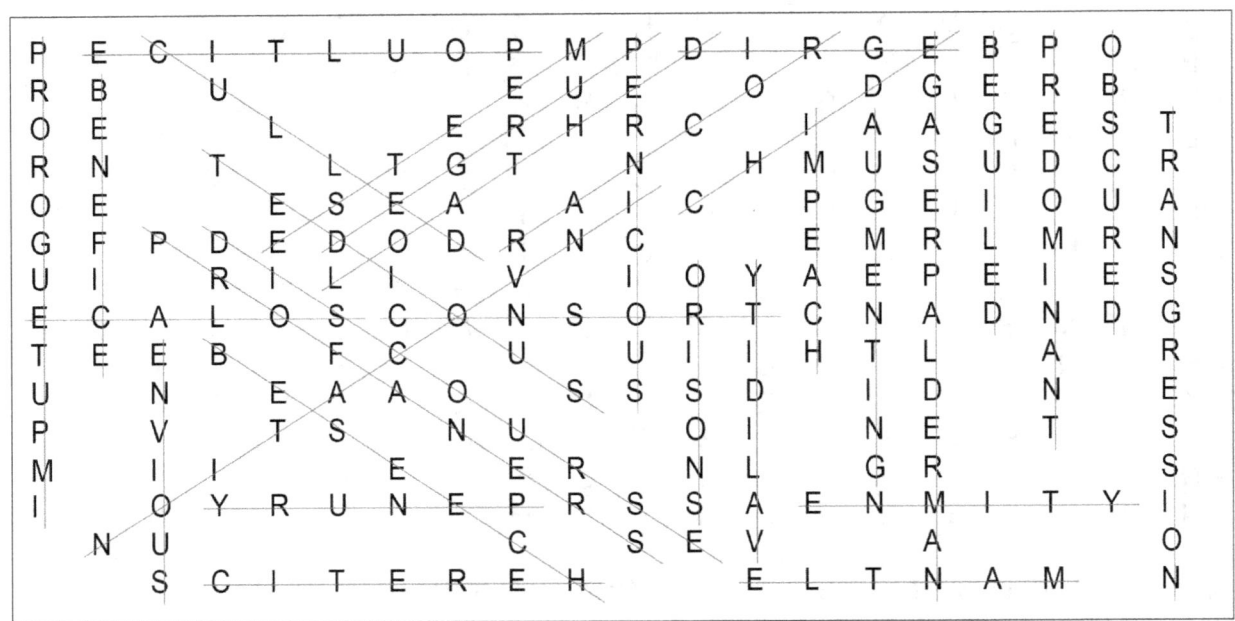

A church office endowed with fixed capital assets (8)
A companion or partner (7)
A member of the municipal legislative body (8)
A soft, moist mass of bread, meal or clay (8)
An omen (7)
Bitterness (6)
Challenge the validity of something (7)
Cloak; coat (6)
Comfort in sorrow (6)
Deceived by guile (8)
Deep seated, often mutual hatred (6)
Destitution (6)
Discontinue a session (8)
Disliked (7)
Evil; wicked (10)
Express disapproval (5)
Freed from impurities (6)
Funeral hymn or lament (5)

Gathered; collected (6)
Good health; how sound something is (8)
Incantation used in conjuring (10)
Indistinctly heard; partially hidden from the senses (8)
Jealous (7)
Making something already developed greater (10)
Most common or conspicuous (11)
Moving or progressing very slowly (7)
Narrate or discuss (9)
Person who holds opinions contrary to the beliefs of others in a group (7)
Prayers (7)
Regard with respect (6)
Request earnestly (7)
Those showing irreverence for what is sacred (9)
To attribute; to credit (6)
Violation of a law (13)

VOCABULARY CROSSWORD PUZZLE - *Romeo and Juliet*

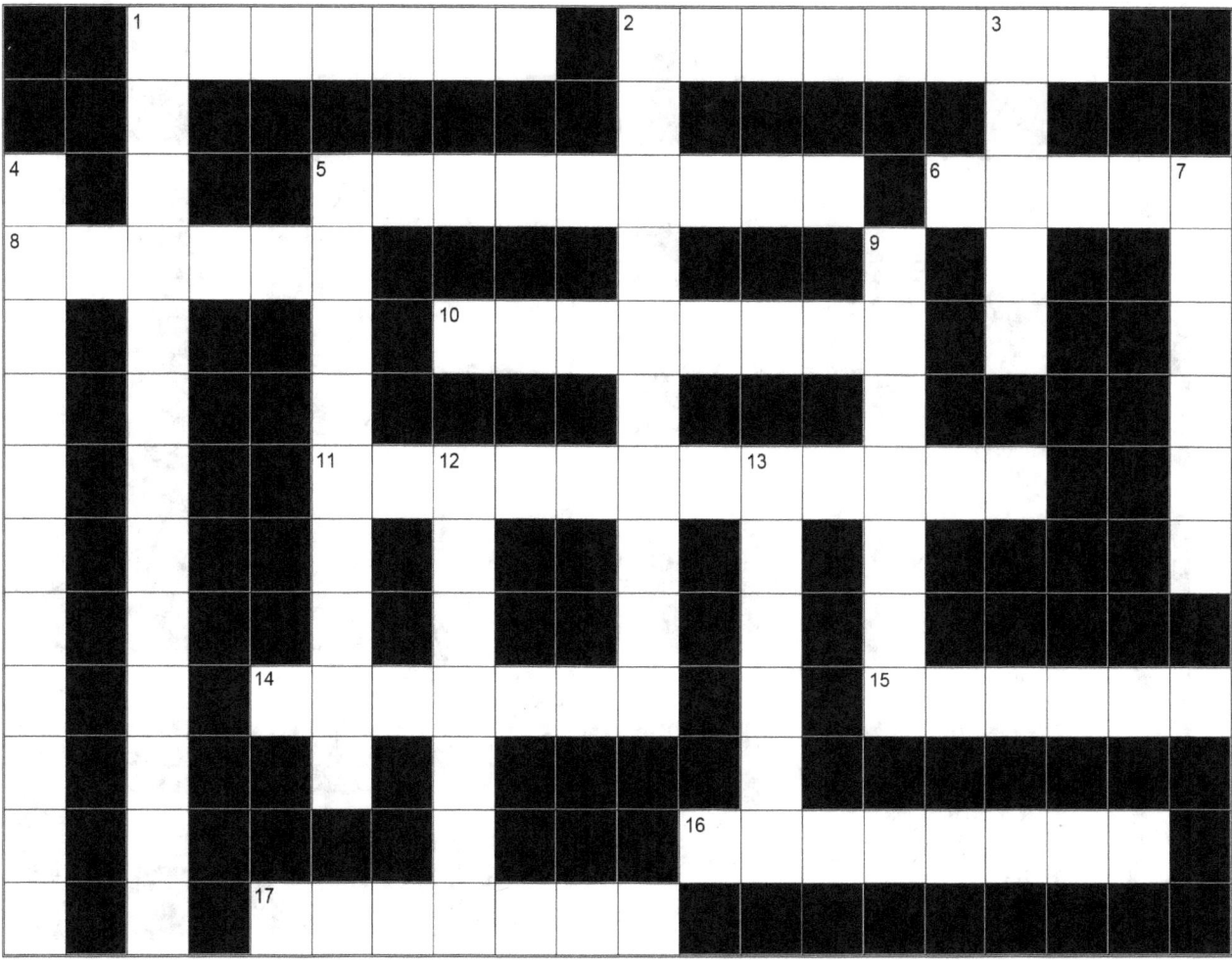

Across
1. Moving or progressing very slowly
2. A soft, moist mass of bread, meal or clay
5. Future generations
6. Funeral hymn or lament
8. Bitterness
10. A member of the municipal legislative body
11. Belonging to as a proper function or part
14. Prayers
15. Comfort in sorrow
16. Deceived by guile
17. Person who holds opinions contrary to the beliefs of others in a group

Down
1. Violation of a law
2. Foreboding
3. Express disapproval
4. Negotiating differences through an impartial third party
5. Those showing irreverence for what is sacred
7. Regard with respect
9. Jealous
12. An omen
13. To attribute; to credit

VOCABULARY CROSSWORD PUZZLE ANSWER KEY - *Romeo and Juliet*

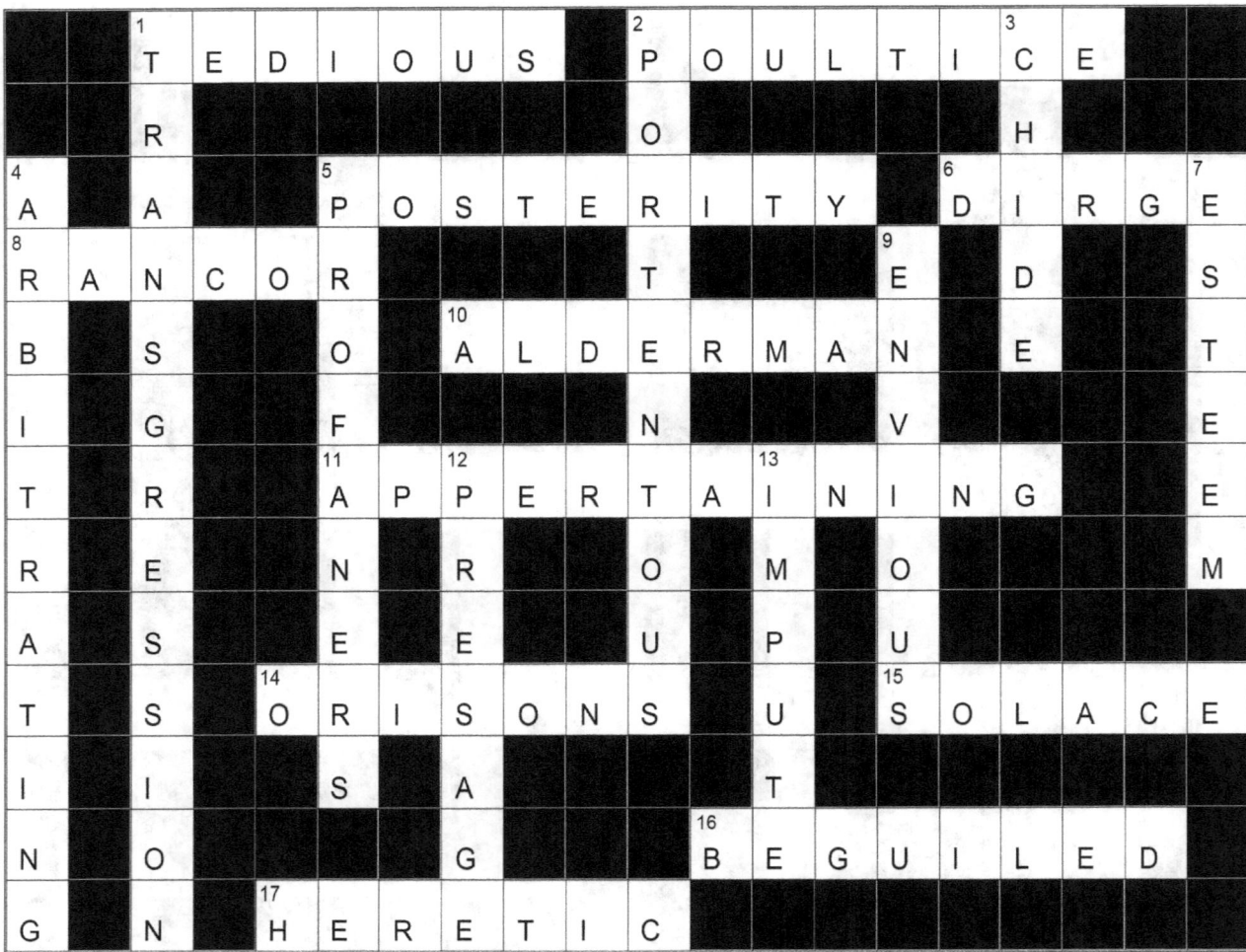

Across
1. Moving or progressing very slowly
2. A soft, moist mass of bread, meal or clay
5. Future generations
6. Funeral hymn or lament
8. Bitterness
10. A member of the municipal legislative body
11. Belonging to as a proper function or part
14. Prayers
15. Comfort in sorrow
16. Deceived by guile
17. Person who holds opinions contrary to the beliefs of others in a group

Down
1. Violation of a law
2. Foreboding
3. Express disapproval
4. Negotiating differences through an impartial third party
5. Those showing irreverence for what is sacred
7. Regard with respect
9. Jealous
12. An omen
13. To attribute; to credit

VOCABULARY WORKSHEET 1 - Romeo and Juliet

___ 1. INVOCATION   A. Jealous
___ 2. LOATHED   B. Foreboding
___ 3. PRESAGE   C. To attribute; to credit
___ 4. ALDERMAN   D. Disliked
___ 5. BESEECH   E. Making something already developed greater
___ 6. PERNICIOUS   F. A member of the municipal legislative body
___ 7. ENVIOUS   G. Moving or progressing very slowly
___ 8. AUGMENTING   H. Iincantation used in conjuring
___ 9. PREDOMINANT   I. Evil; wicked
___ 10. TRANSGRESSION   J. Future generations
___ 11. POSTERITY   K. An omen
___ 12. PORTENTOUS   L. Cloak; coat
___ 13. APPERTAINING   M. Be or become weak or feeble
___ 14. VALIDITY   N. Prayers
___ 15. LAMENTABLE   O. Deceived by guile
___ 16. IMPUTE   P. Request earnestly
___ 17. ARBITRATING   Q. A companion or partner
___ 18. LANGUISH   R. Funeral hymn or lament
___ 19. DIRGE   S. Violation of a law
___ 20. CONSORT   T. Express disapproval
___ 21. MANTLE   U. Causing grief
___ 22. TEDIOUS   V. Of sound health; robust
___ 23. BEGUILED   W. Most common or conspicuous
___ 24. CHIDE   X. Negotiating differences through an impartial third party
___ 25. ORISONS   Y. Belonging to as a proper function or part

KEY: VOCABULARY WORKSHEET 1 - Romeo and Juliet

H -	1. INVOCATION	A. Jealous
D -	2. LOATHED	B. Foreboding
K -	3. PRESAGE	C. To attribute; to credit
F -	4. ALDERMAN	D. Disliked
P -	5. BESEECH	E. Making something already developed greater
I -	6. PERNICIOUS	F. A member of the municipal legislative body
A -	7. ENVIOUS	G. Moving or progressing very slowly
E -	8. AUGMENTING	H. Iincantation used in conjuring
W -	9. PREDOMINANT	I. Evil; wicked
S -	10. TRANSGRESSION	J. Future generations
J -	11. POSTERITY	K. An omen
B -	12. PORTENTOUS	L. Cloak; coat
Y -	13. APPERTAINING	M. Be or become weak or feeble
V -	14. VALIDITY	N. Prayers
U -	15. LAMENTABLE	O. Deceived by guile
C -	16. IMPUTE	P. Request earnestly
X -	17. ARBITRATING	Q. A companion or partner
M -	18. LANGUISH	R. Funeral hymn or lament
R -	19. DIRGE	S. Violation of a law
Q -	20. CONSORT	T. Express disapproval
L -	21. MANTLE	U. Causing grief
G -	22. TEDIOUS	V. Of sound health; robust
O -	23. BEGUILED	W. Most common or conspicuous
T -	24. CHIDE	X. Negotiating differences through an impartial third party
N -	25. ORISONS	Y. Belonging to as a proper function or part

VOCABULARY WORKSHEET 2 - Romeo and Juliet

___ 1. LANGUISH   A. Discontinue a session
___ 2. CHIDE   B. Be or become weak or feeble
___ 3. CONSORT   C. Belonging to as a proper function or part
___ 4. INUNDATION   D. Moving or progressing very slowly
___ 5. VALIDITY   E. Indistinctly heard; faint
___ 6. INVOCATION   F. Cloak; coat
___ 7. POSTERITY   G. Deceived by guile
___ 8. POULTICE   H. Narrate or discuss
___ 9. ARBITRATING   I. Of sound health; robust
___ 10. MANTLE   J. Causing grief
___ 11. LAMENTABLE   K. Gathered; collected
___ 12. CULLED   L. Iincantation used in conjuring
___ 13. ESTEEM   M. Covering with water
___ 14. ORISONS   N. Prayers
___ 15. OBSCURED   O. Disliked
___ 16. LOATHED   P. Future generations
___ 17. DIRGE   Q. Express disapproval
___ 18. DISCOURSE   R. Jealous
___ 19. ENVIOUS   S. Evil; wicked
___ 20. TEDIOUS   T. Funeral hymn or lament
___ 21. SOLACE   U. Negotiating differences through an impartial third party
___ 22. BEGUILED   V. A soft, moist mass of bread, meal or clay
___ 23. APPERTAINING   W. Regard with respect
___ 24. PROROGUE   X. Comfort in sorrow
___ 25. PERNICIOUS   Y. A companion or partner

KEY: VOCABULARY WORKSHEET 2 - Romeo and Juliet

B - 1. LANGUISH		A. Discontinue a session
Q - 2. CHIDE		B. Be or become weak or feeble
Y - 3. CONSORT		C. Belonging to as a proper function or part
M - 4. INUNDATION		D. Moving or progressing very slowly
I - 5. VALIDITY		E. Indistinctly heard; faint
L - 6. INVOCATION		F. Cloak; coat
P - 7. POSTERITY		G. Deceived by guile
V - 8. POULTICE		H. Narrate or discuss
U - 9. ARBITRATING		I. Of sound health; robust
F - 10. MANTLE		J. Causing grief
J - 11. LAMENTABLE		K. Gathered; collected
K - 12. CULLED		L. Iincantation used in conjuring
W - 13. ESTEEM		M. Covering with water
N - 14. ORISONS		N. Prayers
E - 15. OBSCURED		O. Disliked
O - 16. LOATHED		P. Future generations
T - 17. DIRGE		Q. Express disapproval
H - 18. DISCOURSE		R. Jealous
R - 19. ENVIOUS		S. Evil; wicked
D - 20. TEDIOUS		T. Funeral hymn or lament
X - 21. SOLACE		U. Negotiating differences through an impartial third party
G - 22. BEGUILED		V. A soft, moist mass of bread, meal or clay
C - 23. APPERTAINING		W. Regard with respect
A - 24. PROROGUE		X. Comfort in sorrow
S - 25. PERNICIOUS		Y. A companion or partner

VOCABULARY JUGGLE LETTER REVIEW GAME CLUES - *Romeo and Juliet*

SCRAMBLED	WORD	CLUE
NMERLDAA	ALDERMAN	a member of the municipal legislative body GN-
MGNTEAIU	AUGMENTING	to make (something already developed) greater
OSORNSI	ORISONS	prayers
REGUPORO	PROROGUE	to discontinue a session
TYDLIVIA	VALIDITY	well grounded
TEIGIANPPNRA	APPERTAINING	to belong as a proper function or part
IEECHSRT	HERETICS	people who hold controversial opinions
ESRAEPG	PRESAGE	an omen
ECHMIAP	IMPEACH	to challenge the validity of something
SOIDUET	TEDIOUS	moving or progressing very slowly
SEOBD	BODES	to be an omen of
UEDCLL	CULLED	gathered; collected
IOIUPESNCR	PERNICIOUS	evil; wicked
HLISGAUN	LANGUISH	to be or become weak or feeble
RTMPNOEINAD	PREDOMINANT	most common or conspicuous
BRNATTIGRIA	ARBITRATING	to submit to settlement or judgment by arbitra-tion
IINTOOVACN	INVOCATION	an incantation used in conjuring
EIBCNEEF	BENEFICE	a church office endowed with fixed capital assets
DNONINAUTI	INUNDATION	covering with water
OASHRB	ABHORS	to reject vehemently
UYPREN	PENURY	destitution
EUPILTOC	POULTICE	a soft, moist mass of bread, meal or clay
NOTRCSO	CONSORT	a companion or partner
SEFNORPAR	PROFANERS	irreverence for what is sacred
GUDEDR	DRUDGE	a person who does tedious or menial work
PTOONUSRET	PORTENTOUS	foreboding
OSUEINV	ENVIOUS	feeling, expressing or characterized by envy
EHCESBE	BESEECH	to request earnestly
TSEOBUSIRO	BOISTEROUS	rough and stormy
YITEMN	ENMITY	deep seated, often mutual hatred
ELAMTN	MANTLE	a cloak
TEEEMS	ESTEEM	regard with respect
SRGIDE	DIRGES	funeral hymns or laments
ERDUGP	PURGED	freed from impurities
EDIGLEUB	BEGUILED	to deceive by guile
OASELC	SOLACE	comfort in sorrow